THINK HISTORY!

REVOLUTIONARY TIMES
1500–1750

Ros Adams   Denise Waugh   Steve Waugh

Series editor: Lindsay von Elbing

heinemann.co.uk
✓ Free online support
✓ Useful weblinks
✓ 24 hour online ordering

01865 888080

Heinemann
Inspiring generations

Heinemann Educational Publishers
Halley Court, Jordan Hill, Oxford, OX2 8EJ
Part of Harcourt Education

Heinemann is the registered trademark of
Harcourt Education Limited

© Ros Adams, Denise Waugh, Steve Waugh, 2003

First published 2003

07 06 05
10 9 8 7 6 5

British Library Cataloguing in Publication Data is available from the British Library on
request.

10 digit ISBN: 0 435 31350 9
13 digit ISBN: 978 0 435313 50 0

Produced by IFA Design Ltd
Printed in Spain by Mateu Cromo s.a.
Original illustrations © Harcourt Education Limited, 2003

Photographic acknowledgements
The authors and publisher would like to thank the following for permission to reproduce
photographs:
AKG: 8A, 24B, 95H, 98D, 152A, 172C; Art Archive: 11A; Bridgeman Art Library: 8B, 23A, 24C,
29A, 30C, 42D, 51B, 57A, 72B, 85B, 95F, 96K, 97A, 100J, 106K, 111A, 120A, 149D, 165C, 197A,
214G; BAL/Bristol City Art Gallery: 19G; BAL/Guildhall: 34C; BAL/Hatfield House: 93A; Bristol
Museum and Art Gallery: 212B; Christopher Ridley: 31G; Corbis: 8C, 94C; Fotomas Index:
48E, 67B, 73C, 175A, 130A, 133A; Glasgow Museums: 184B; Historical Archive: 133B; Hulton
Getty: 79D, 117C; Mansell Collection: 31F; Mary Evans Picture Library: 12B, 35F, 51A, 108P,
135H, 137B, 139E, 140G; National Library of Scotland: 187A; National Maritime Museum:
173E; National Portrait Gallery: 40C, 45A, 203A, 204B; National Trust: 94D, 96I; Palace of
Westminster Collection: 49F; Peter Newark: 148B, 153C, 214E; Rex: 137A; Ronald Grant: 26A;
The Royal Collection: 85A, 191A; Scala: 104H; Scala/Galleria d'Arte Moderna, Florence: 36H;
Science Photo Library: 197B; Sidney Sussex College, Cambridge: 63A; Topham
Picturepoint: 180A; Viscount de L'Isle/Penshurst Palace: 99H

Source unknown: 47C, 51C, 67A, 68C, 69D, 70A, 77A, 80F, 83B, 102B, 109R, 134F, 154F, 179D

Cover photograph: © The Art Archive. The painting is 'The Battle of Marston Moor' by
James Ward.

Picture research by Veneta Bullen

Tel: 01865 888058 www.heinemann.co.uk

CONTENTS

INTRODUCTION

SOURCE A

A contemporary painting of Anne Boleyn.

SOURCE B

A seventeenth-century print of a witch.

SOURCE C

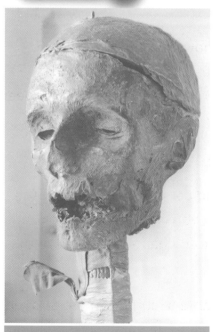

Cromwell's skull on a spike.

💡 Which one of these is the odd one out? Why?

At this stage, you might want to make a wild guess. You might even be able to make an 'educated guess' based on your Key Stage Two study of history, or from your own general knowledge.

One possible answer is that Oliver Cromwell is the odd one out – he's a man and the other two are women. However, there are many more possibilities, and there is not just one correct answer!

The good thing about the game of odd one out is that it makes you *think* about links and connections between things. The more you know about history, the more links and connections you can make. Making links and connections is a very important skill, because the information in this book is organised into three big sections:

1 Religion and internal politics
2 Social life
3 External relations

Quite often, information from one section may overlap with another section, so you will need to think hard! To help you to do this, each big section has its own introduction.

Let's consider the three big sections:

Religion and internal politics

💡 Do you remember finding out about life in the Middle Ages? You probably recall that religion was very important at that time. Can you suggest why?

Between 1500 and 1750 religious beliefs changed a great deal. The picture of Anne Boleyn was chosen to represent religious changes. Turn to pages 6 to 7 and skim read. Can you work out what connects Anne Boleyn with religious changes?

Social life

This theme is to do with how different groups of people in England lived. One of the most interesting events of this period was the witch craze of the seventeenth century.

External relations

Finally, we also need to find out about how England got on with other countries between 1500 and 1750. Cromwell's picture was chosen because he was involved controversially with events between England and Ireland in the seventeenth century.

In the same way that you made links and connections between the three figures in the odd one out activity, you can also make links between the themes. For example, religious changes affected both social life and external relations.

By the end of this book, you should be able to suggest more answers to the odd one out puzzle at the beginning. For a real challenge, you may even want to think about how the information in the book has been organised into three sections. Would you organise the information differently?

THEME: RELIGION AND INTERNAL POLITICS

INTRODUCTION

How many people in your class believe in God? How many attend a Christian place of worship regularly? The answers to these questions today are often 'very few'. In the sixteenth and seventeenth centuries it would have been very different. Every English person would have believed in a Christian God and would have attended church regularly. Religion was a vital part of their lives. It was so important that it changed the history of Britain on a number of occasions.

Henry VIII was so determined to get a divorce that he broke away from the authority of the Pope. In the following reigns people's extreme views about religion led to violence and bloodshed. Catholics burned Protestants and Protestants executed so-called Catholic 'spies'. Henry's daughter, Mary, was given the nickname 'Bloody Mary' because she burned many Protestants in her short reign (1553-8). But did she really deserve the name?

Mary, Queen of Scots, found that being a Catholic brought her into conflict with her cousin, Queen Elizabeth I of England - a Protestant. Mary spent almost twenty years in prison in England, from 1568 to 1587 - and then Elizabeth had her executed. Did she deserve such a fate?

In the seventeenth century King James I (1603-25), a Protestant, faced opposition from the Catholics. Did Guy Fawkes really try to blow him up in the Gunpowder Plot - or was he framed? King James I's grandson, James II, was a Catholic, but within three years of becoming king he had become so unpopular that the so-called 'Glorious Revolution' of 1688 forced him to flee into exile. How 'glorious' was this revolution really?

Religion even contributed to the outbreak of the Civil War in 1642, when King Charles I fought parliament for control of England.

When the Civil War was over, the king was executed and religious extremists called Puritans ran the country.

Religion and arguments over religion led to many changes in England in the sixteenth and seventeenth centuries - changes in politics, family life, employment, leisure activities, dress, behaviour - in fact to changes in every aspect of people's lives, regardless of whether they were rich or poor, male or female, Protestant or Catholic. They truly were Revolutionary Times!

TIMELINE 1517-1685

1517	Martin Luther launches a major protest against the Catholic Church.
1527	Henry VIII asks the Pope for a divorce. It is refused.
1534	Henry VIII becomes Head of the Church of England.
1536	Henry VIII orders all the monasteries in England to be closed.
1547-54	Edward VI tries to make England Protestant.
1554-8	Mary I tries to make England Catholic.
1558	Elizabeth I becomes queen and tries to find a 'middle way' in religion.
1567	Rebellion in Scotland against the Catholic Mary, Queen of Scots.
1587	Mary, Queen of Scots is beheaded at Fotheringay Castle.
1603	James VI of Scotland, son of Mary, Queen of Scots, succeeds Elizabeth I and becomes James I of England.
1605	Catholics try to blow up James I and Parliament in the Gunpowder Plot.
1625	James I dies and is succeeded by Charles I.
1629-40	Charles I rules without Parliament.
1642-9	The English Civil War.
1649	Trial and execution of Charles I.
1652	The Puritan Parliament bans the celebration of Christmas.
1658	Death of Oliver Cromwell.
1660	Charles II returns from exile. Puritans lose their influence.
1685	Charles II dies and is succeeded by his brother James II.

1

DID ENGLAND BECOME PROTESTANT IN THE SIXTEENTH CENTURY?

WHY DID HENRY VIII BREAK AWAY FROM THE AUTHORITY OF THE POPE?

Objectives

By the end of this section you will find out:
- why Henry VIII wanted a divorce from Catherine of Aragon
- why Henry's desire for a divorce led to a break with the Pope and the Roman Catholic Church.

You will be able to:
- identify examples of cause and effect in the events leading to the break with the Pope and the Roman Catholic Church.

Key words

Heir The next person in line to succeed a king or queen.

Starter

It is 1527. You are Henry VIII and you have a problem.

*You have been married for almost 20 years to Catherine of Aragon. She has given you a daughter, but no son has survived infancy. You want a male **heir**. Catherine is too old to have any more children but you are not. You have fallen in love with Anne Boleyn, who is 20 years old, and you want to marry her.*

 *What would you do if you were in Henry VIII's position?*

SOURCE (A)

Catherine of Aragon.

SOURCE (B)

King Henry VIII of England.

SOURCE (C)

Anne Boleyn.

Possible answers to Henry's problem		
1 Ask the **Pope** for a divorce.	**2** Execute Catherine and marry Anne.	**3** Wait until Catherine dies and then marry Anne.
Possible results of these actions		
A Catherine may outlive you, and if Anne becomes pregnant outside of marriage your child (possibly the son you've been waiting for) will be born **illegitimate** – and therefore won't be able to succeed you as king.	**B** The Pope allowed you to marry Catherine in the first place – perhaps he'll let you divorce her. But Catherine's nephew, Emperor Charles V, is holding the Pope captive. It is unlikely that he will agree to the shame of his aunt being divorced.	**C** Catherine is very popular with the English people – divorcing or executing her would make you very unpopular. Anyway, she hasn't committed a crime.

💡 *Which course of action was likely to produce which result?*

💡 *What advice do you think Henry received from his ministers?*

Why did the problem of Henry's divorce lead to a break with the Pope and the Roman Catholic Church?

Henry's wife, Catherine, had previously been married to his brother, Arthur. Arthur had died after only four months of marriage to Catherine, and Henry had then married Catherine. Catherine had given birth to several children by Henry, but only one child – a daughter, Mary – had survived infancy. Henry was desperate for a son. He began to believe that God was punishing him for marrying his brother's widow – something the Bible said was wrong. Henry asked the Pope for a divorce, but was refused.

Key words

Pope The head of the Catholic Church, who lives in Rome.
Illegitimate A person who is born to parents who are not married.
Archbishop of Canterbury The leading churchman in England.

As time went on Henry became more desperate. He finally decided to break from the Pope's authority as Head of the Roman Catholic Church and to make himself Head of the Church of England. This meant that Henry would no longer need to seek the Pope's approval for any decisions he made. The **Archbishop of Canterbury**, Thomas Cranmer, could now declare Henry's marriage to Catherine unlawful and grant him his divorce.

This was a good thing for Henry because he had already secretly married Anne Boleyn, who was pregnant. The new marriage was declared legal and Anne was crowned Queen. Three months later Anne gave birth … to a girl.

💡 How do you think Henry felt when Anne gave birth to a daughter?

TASKS…

Many of the causes of Henry VIII's break with the Pope are closely linked.

1 Work in pairs. In your book, copy the boxes below and draw arrows between two boxes to show how one fact led to another. You must be able to use the words 'and so' to link the two. **WS**

Your objective is to get to the box in the middle, while trying to make as many links as you can along the way. You may draw as many arrows as you like, as long as the second box happens as a result of the first.

Henry wanted a male heir.

Henry wanted a divorce from Catherine of Aragon.

Henry believed his marriage to Catherine was sinful.

The Pope wouldn't grant Henry a divorce.

HENRY VIII BROKE WITH THE POPE

Henry made himself Head of the Church in England.

Anne became pregnant.

Henry married Anne.

Catherine could not produce a male heir.

The Pope was a prisoner of Catherine's nephew.

2 When you have finished, compare your decisions with another pair. Who can explain the most links?

3 Use your diagram to write a paragraph explaining why Henry VIII broke with the Pope and the Roman Catholic Church.

Plenary

Here are the answers! Work out the questions.

1 Catherine had previously been married to Henry's brother, Arthur.
2 The Pope.
3 Henry decided to make himself Head of the Church in England.
4 Henry wanted his son to be legitimate.
5 Archbishop Cranmer.

WHAT WAS WRONG WITH THE CATHOLIC CHURCH IN THE SIXTEENTH CENTURY?

Objectives

By the end of this section, you will understand:
- why a growing number of people were unhappy with the Catholic Church in the sixteenth century
- why Protestants objected to the Catholic Church.

You will be able to:
- explain the main differences between Catholic and Protestant ideas.

Starter

SOURCE A

Coins from the reigns of Henry VIII, Edward VI, Mary I and Elizabeth I.

What do these coins have in common?

Look carefully at the inscription on each coin and you will see that it contains the abbreviation F.D. or 'Fid. Def.' – Fidei Defensor. This is Latin for 'Defender of the Faith'.

Look at a modern coin and read the inscription. What meaning do you think it has today?

Criticism of the Catholic Church

In 1521 Henry VIII was given the title *Fidei Defensor* by the Pope as a reward for his loyalty in defending the Catholic Church against criticism from a growing protest movement in Europe. Henry had written an attack on these 'Protestants' and the Pope had rewarded Henry by granting him the title. Henry was so pleased that he had *Fidei Defensor* put on all new coins.

However, only a few years later in 1533, Henry was himself in a bitter argument with the Pope over his divorce and broke from the Pope's authority as Head of the Catholic Church. Parliament now made Henry Head of the Church in England.

What was the new protest movement all about?

In 1517 a German monk called Martin Luther made a list of 95 complaints about the Catholic Church. He was particularly annoyed because a friar named Johann Tetzel had come to his town to sell indulgences. These were certificates which said that your sins were forgiven and so you could get into heaven. Luther was angry because

Martin Luther.

he did not believe it was possible to buy your way into heaven. He knew that Tetzel was just raising money so that the Pope could spend more and more money on beautiful buildings in Rome. Luther felt that this was one of the many ways in which the Catholic Church was not behaving in a Christian manner, and that he had to protest.

It was dangerous to criticise the Catholic Church openly. Luther could have been arrested and charged with being a **heretic**. The penalty for this was death – many people had been sentenced to burning for **heresy** in the past. However, Luther was lucky. The ruler of his state, Prince Frederick the Wise, agreed with Luther's criticism of indulgences and decided to protect him. Luther's ideas spread quickly and soon his followers, or Protestants, as they became known, began to start churches of their own.

What did it mean to be a Catholic in England at this time?

For most people at the beginning of the sixteenth century, the Catholic religion did not just happen in church. It was a huge part of their lives. God, Jesus, the angels, heaven, hell and the devil were all very real to them, and the village church was the centre of their lives.

Key words

Heretic A person who follows beliefs which are against the teachings of the established Church.
Heresy Beliefs which are against the accepted religion.

People went to church services at least once every Sunday and often during the week as well. They found the **ritual** of the church service comforting. The priest conducted **Mass** at the altar and read to them from the Bible in Latin – a language they did not understand. It seemed very powerful and mysterious.

The priest was people's link to God and he told them Bible stories which were often illustrated by colourful pictures on the wall or in the stained-glass windows of the church. **Incense** was burned and it was thought that a miracle took place at every Mass, when the wine and bread turned into the flesh and blood of Jesus. **Relics** would help people get closer to God if they touched them.

Why was the priest such an important person to Catholics?

What were the differences between Catholic and Protestant ideas?

Catholics and Protestants are both Christians, but in the sixteenth century it was very important to people exactly *what* they believed about God and Jesus and *how* they worshipped. Each side was sure that theirs was the right religion and that the followers of the other religion would burn in hell for their beliefs. It was clearly very important that as many people as possible followed the *right* religion. Both sides were prepared to punish or even kill the followers of the other religion in order to make sure that this happened.

> ### Key words
>
> **Ritual** Religious ceremony.
> **Mass** A religious ceremony which celebrates the Last Supper of Jesus.
> **Incense** Material which is burned to give off a perfumed smoke, often used in religious ceremonies.
> **Relic** A holy object, often a souvenir of a saint such as bones, clothes or possessions.

TASKS...

1 a) Look at the statements A to P.

A   *People should glorify God by decorating churches with ornaments, statues and stained glass windows.*

B   *There is no such thing as a miracle. Relics are just superstition and should have no part in the worship of God.*

C   *People need to understand church services and the Bible, so they should be in English.*

D   *Priests should be different from ordinary people. They have a special job and should dedicate themselves to the Church and not get married.*

TASKS...

E   Doing good works will help you to get into heaven – or you can buy an indulgence.

F   The Pope is only human. Jesus is the head of the Church and only He can forgive your sins.

G   People shouldn't be distracted when worshipping God. Churches should be plain and simple.

H   No miracle occurs during Mass. Jesus is present in the wine and bread, but they do not change into his flesh and blood. The ceremony should be called 'communion'.

I   Latin makes the Bible and services special. It has been the language of the Church for hundreds of years.

J   People can speak to God themselves. They do not need a priest to do it for them and they should be allowed to take part in church services.

K   Relics are important as they can help you get nearer to God. Sometimes they can produce miracles.

L   A good preacher can help people to understand Bible stories and can explain things to them, but he does not need to be set apart – he should get married.

M   The priest is very important. He is there to link ordinary people with God. He should conduct the service for ordinary people.

N   Trying to bribe your way into heaven will not work. God has already chosen those who will be saved from the fires of hell.

O   It is important to obey the Pope. He is God's representative on earth and his priests can help you to get your sins forgiven more quickly when you die.

P   During Mass a miracle occurs and the wine and bread change into Jesus's flesh and blood.

b) Now look at the drawings showing the insides of a Catholic church and a Protestant church (page 15).

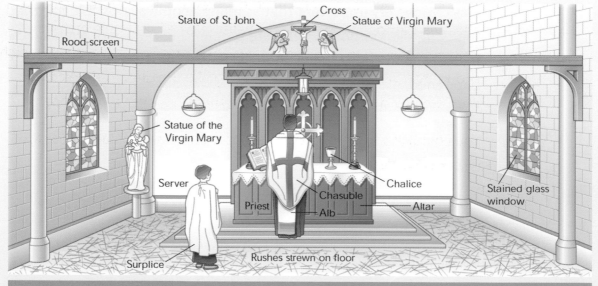

Statue of St John — Cross — Statue of Virgin Mary

Rood screen

Statue of the Virgin Mary

Server

Priest

Chasuble

Alb

Chalice

Altar

Stained glass window

Surplice

Rushes strewn on floor

The inside of a Catholic church.

TASKS...

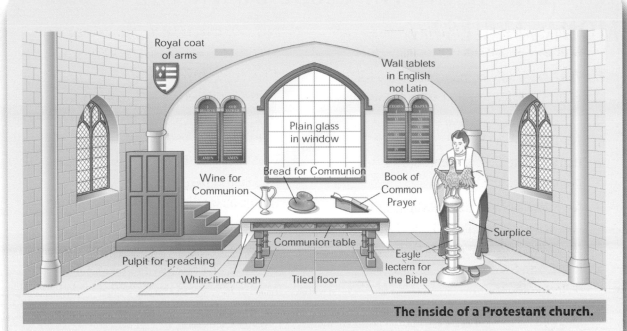

Royal coat of arms

Wall tablets in English not Latin

Plain glass in window

Bread for Communion

Wine for Communion

Book of Common Prayer

Surplice

Communion table

Eagle lectern for the Bible

Pulpit for preaching

White linen cloth

Tiled floor

The inside of a Protestant church.

c) Draw a table with two columns. At the top of one column, put 'Catholic Church'. At the top of the other, put 'Protestant Church'. Now, try to sort the statements according to whether they describe Catholic or Protestant beliefs. Write the letters of each statement in the correct column. **WS**

Plenary

How many ways can you think of to remember the differences between Catholic and Protestant beliefs? Here is a simple memory jogger to help you: 'Pure Protestants and Complicated Catholics', which shows that the Protestants wanted to make the Church simple, while the Catholics wanted to keep all the ornaments and decorations.

You could also try mnemonics or a poem or song, or make up a story with key words in it.

WHY DID HENRY VIII CLOSE DOWN THE MONASTERIES?

Objectives

By the end of this section you will know:
- why Henry VIII closed down the monasteries in England
- what was thought to be wrong with the monasteries
- how the monasteries were closed down
- why many people were concerned about the **dissolution** of the monasteries
- how Henry dealt with the Pilgrimage of Grace and why he took such harsh action against it.

Starter

In the sixteenth century, which one of the following do you think would have been the odd one out:

- *a hotel*
- *a prison*
- *a hospital*
- *a meditation centre*
- *a school?*

Here is a clue! All but one of the functions would have been carried out in monasteries.

What led to the dissolution of the monasteries?

Henry's divorce was not the only problem he had. Although he had made himself Head of the Church of England and had stopped sending **taxes** to the Pope, Henry was still spending far too much money. Henry was very extravagant. He liked the finer things in life – wearing fine clothes and hosting impressive parties. He had also fought a long and costly war with France. After Henry broke with the Pope he was also worried that the Catholic countries of Europe might attack England.

 How could Henry get more money and also make sure that he didn't have powerful enemies?

REVOLUTIONARY TIMES 1500–1750

Many people thought the break with the Pope was wrong, much to Henry's annoyance. Most monks and nuns were loyal to the Pope as leader of the Catholic Church, not the king. Henry wanted everyone to be loyal to him. He even executed his old friend, Sir Thomas More, because he would not accept Henry as Head of the Church of England.

Henry also needed money, and so in 1536 he instructed his chief minister, Thomas Cromwell, to start closing down the monasteries. Over the years, many monks had begun to ignore their **vows** of **poverty** and **chastity** and now lived very comfortable lives. Many monasteries had grown rich and owned a great deal of land. They had gold crosses and cups, beautiful pictures and statues, richly embroidered cloths and expensive Bibles. Even the buildings themselves were valuable – the lead on the roof was worth a lot of money.

Monasteries, however, were not simply corrupt. They played a very important role in the life of the country. They acted as hotels – at a time when such things didn't exist – giving travellers food and shelter. They also acted as schools, teachings boys how to read and write, and as hospitals, looking after the sick and needy at a time when few people could afford the services of a doctor.

Key words

Vow A promise which states a person will behave in a certain way.
Poverty Being poor. Monks took a vow of poverty as a sign of their religious devotion.
Chastity Being pure of body, which includes not having sexual intercourse.

Corruption within the Church in England

Because closing down the monasteries would be unpopular with many people, Henry VIII and Thomas Cromwell needed a good excuse to close them down. So Cromwell sent inspectors round the country to report on the state of the monasteries. He asked the inspectors to report on how pure the monks and nuns were in their religious practices and how wealthy the monasteries were. Cromwell chose inspectors who were not loyal Catholics.

- Before you read extracts from the reports, have a go at predicting what the reports might say.

- Do you think the inspectors' reports on the monasteries would be fair?

What can we tell about the state of the monasteries from historical evidence?

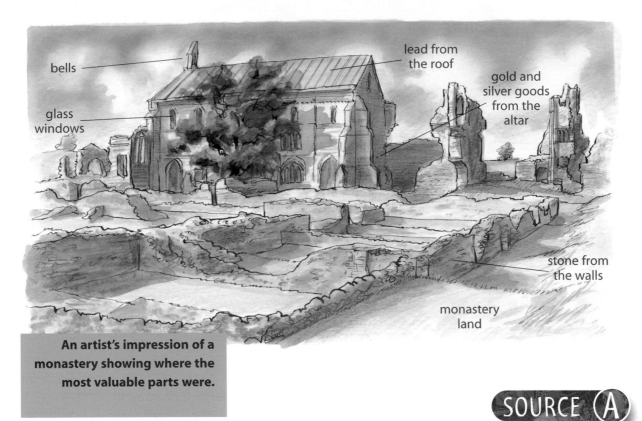

bells

glass windows

lead from the roof

gold and silver goods from the altar

stone from the walls

monastery land

An artist's impression of a monastery showing where the most valuable parts were.

Key words

Habit A monk's robe.
Celibate Living as a single person and not having sexual relations.

Monks and nuns were supposed to live like Jesus's disciples. They should:

- give all their possessions away and live in poverty
- wear a basic **habit** and eat simple food
- stay **celibate**
- look after the poor, the sick and travellers
- behave in a Christian manner
- worship and pray several times a day
- copy passages from the Bible.

An extract from a modern history book.

SOURCE B

I could not find anything bad about the convent, no matter how hard I tried. I believe this was because everybody had got together and agreed to keep the convent's secrets. Among the relics were the coals that St Lawrence was burnt upon, the clippings of St Edmund's nails, St Thomas of Canterbury's penknife and his boots, and enough pieces of the Holy Cross to make a whole cross.

An extract from the report on St Edmund's convent.

SOURCE C

Found the **Prior** at that time in bed with a woman, both naked, about 11 o'clock in the morning.

An extract from the report on Crossed Friars monastery in London.

SOURCE D

The abbot delighted much at playing at dice and spent a lot of money on it. Women frequently came into this monastery.

An extract from the report on St Edmund's abbey.

SOURCE E

I will tell your Grace something about the monks in my monastery, and how little notice is taken of King Henry's command that any mention of the Pope should be crossed out of all our books. The monks drink and play bowls after breakfast till ten o'clock or midday. They come to morning service drunk. They do nothing for the love of God. They have many other faults which I have no time to tell you about.

An extract from a letter dated 1535 from Richard Beereley, a monk, to Thomas Cromwell.

SOURCE F

Priories were offered at bargain prices, and loyalty to Henry as Head of the English Church was gained through bricks and mortar. And by filling the Crown's **coffers** with the proceeds, the dissolution gave Henry the means to stand up to the worst the Catholic powers could throw at him.

Adapted from *A History of Britain*, by Simon Schama, published in 2000.

Key words

Prior The title given to the head monk in a priory.
Priories Religious houses like monasteries.
Coffers Boxes for holding money.

SOURCE G

A nineteenth century painting showing inspectors closing down a monastery.

TASKS...

1 Copy out the table below.
Use Sources A–G to complete the table showing the reasons why Henry VIII closed down the monasteries.

2 Source E was not written by an inspector. It was written by a monk. Does that surprise you in any way? Does it make you believe the inspectors' reports, or do you think the monk was biased? Explain your reasons.

	Source	Evidence
The monks and nuns were not following the rules of their religious houses.		
Monks and nuns still supported the Pope.		
Henry VIII needed to get the support of the nobility.		
Henry VIII needed money in case of a war against him by Catholic countries.		

What was the Pilgrimage of Grace?

Many people, especially in the north of England, rebelled against the closure of monasteries. The rebels were also angry about rumours that some churches were to be closed. Nobles, gentlemen, monks and lawyers leading thousands of ordinary people swore their loyalty to the king and called their movement the 'Pilgrimage of Grace'.

The uprising was so big that at first Henry could do nothing but agree to talk to the rebel leaders. He called some of them to London, including their spokesman, Robert Aske. Henry promised to look into their complaints and many of the rebels then went home.

Henry did not like people to challenge him and started to build up his army. When he felt strong enough to strike back he invited Aske to more talks. He immediately arrested him and the other leaders. Henry was completely ruthless when people opposed him.

Aske was tried and then hanged in chains from the walls of York Castle so that people would learn a lesson. Churches were not closed, but Henry continued the work of dissolving the monasteries. Any monks who disobeyed his orders were hanged.

What was Henry's attitude towards translating the Bible into English?

Henry might have broken away from the Pope's authority but he continued to follow the Catholic religion. He agreed to let the Bible be translated into English in 1539 and ordered that a copy should be placed in every church in England. However, he quickly became worried that because more people could read the Bible in English it would lead to too much discussion about religion. Henry therefore ordered Parliament to pass a law forbidding 'women, apprentices, serving men and labourers' from reading the Bible themselves. But it was too late. The new printing presses had already made it possible for ordinary people to own their own copy.

Why might Henry have been worried about people discussing religion?

Why do you think that 'women, apprentices, serving men and labourers' were forbidden to read the Bible?

TASKS...

1 Write down two things that the Pilgrimage of Grace tells us about each of the following:
   a) Henry as a king?
   b) Henry's attitude towards religion?

2 What do Henry's actions over the English Bible tell us about his attitude towards religion?

Plenary

Which three of the five statements below do you think best sum up why Henry VIII wanted the monasteries closed?

- Henry VIII was very greedy and needed more money for his extravagant lifestyle.
- Henry VIII needed lots of money in case he was attacked by the Catholic countries of Europe.
- Henry VIII needed to make sure the nobles of England supported him. The best way to do this was to give them land and money.
- Many monks still obeyed the Pope's commands rather than Henry's and the king thought this was dangerous.
- Many monks were not following the ideas on which their monasteries had been founded. They were not living holy lives, but sinful ones.

Is one of the three you have chosen more important than the others? Explain your answer.

Explain your choice to a partner. Do you both agree? If you don't, try to persuade each other that you are right by using the evidence to support your case.

DID ELIZABETH I FIND A 'MIDDLE WAY' IN RELIGION?

Objectives

By the end of this section you will know:

- how religion had changed by the end of Elizabeth I's reign
- why Elizabeth changed religion in England.

You will be able to:

- explain how Elizabeth's changes represented a 'middle way' in religion
- answer the big question: did England become Protestant in the sixteenth century?

Starter

protestantism

Try to work out which of the following is the odd one out:

- *the Pope*
- *Henry VIII*
- *Martin Luther*
- *Robert Aske.*

Discuss your choice with someone else in your class. There could be more than one correct answer.

How did Edward VI and Mary I change religion in England?

 SOURCE **A**

Henry VIII's son and heir, Edward, was born to his third wife, Jane Seymour, in 1537. Even though he was a Catholic, Henry allowed Edward to be educated by Protestants. Edward was only 9 years old when Henry VIII died in 1547, so was too young to rule by himself. The result was that Edward's Protestant advisers started to make England a truly Protestant country.

The religious changes under Edward VI probably had little effect on most people. Those living in villages carried on worshipping in the same way as they always had. In the larger towns, however, much more changed.

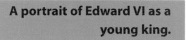
A portrait of Edward VI as a young king.

💡 What do you think would have happened in churches to make them Protestant?

SOURCE B

A portrait of Mary I.

SOURCE C

A portrait of Elizabeth I when she first became queen in 1558.

Key words

Legitimate Born to parents who are married.

At the age of 15 Edward VI died and Henry's elder daughter, Mary Tudor, became queen. As the daughter of Catherine of Aragon, Mary was a strict Catholic. She hated the religious changes which had taken place during her brother's reign and set about reversing them immediately.

💡 What do you think would have happened in churches to make them Catholic?

Mary I was 39 years old when she became Queen of England and she wanted to achieve a great deal. She married a Catholic, Prince Philip of Spain, and set about making sure that all traces of Protestantism in England were wiped out. Some people were very unhappy about this and wanted the Church to stay Protestant. Mary decided that if people would not willingly go back to being Catholic, she would burn them for their heresy. More than 200 people may have died in this way for their beliefs.

Mary I died childless after only four years as queen. She was succeeded by her half-sister, Elizabeth, who was Anne Boleyn's daughter. Elizabeth reigned from 1558 until 1603.

What was Elizabeth's 'middle way' in religion?

To Catholics, Elizabeth was illegitimate. This was because, in the eyes of the Catholic Church, the Pope had not granted Henry his divorce and so Henry had really been married to Catherine of Aragon at the time of Elizabeth's birth. As far as Catholics were concerned, Elizabeth therefore had no right to the throne.

Protestants, on the other hand, believed that Elizabeth was **legitimate**. They did not want another Catholic monarch like Mary I and hoped that Elizabeth would give her full backing to the Protestant Church.

However, Elizabeth knew that many of her subjects were loyal Catholics and she did not want to turn them against her. She would need their support, otherwise the Pope and the other Catholic rulers of Europe would never accept her as Queen of England. Indeed, the Pope even said that if a Catholic killed Elizabeth, that person would be forgiven by God.

 What could Elizabeth I do to win the support of her Catholic subjects?

TASKS...

1 a) Copy the table below. It describes the actions Elizabeth took to create a 'middle way' in religion that she hoped all English people could accept. **WS**

b) Using a highlighter pen, colour all the actions which Protestants would have liked.

c) In a different colour, highlight all the actions which the Catholics would have liked.

d) If both Protestants and Catholics would have liked them, colour the actions half and half.

• Have a prayer book (setting out the service) in English, written by Thomas Cranmer. • Have the traditional order of service. • Have a few pictures and statues in churches. • Don't have the Pope as Head of the Church of England.	• Have bishops in charge of priests. • Keep all the old churches. • Have priests read from the English Bible in church. • Fine those who refused to go to church.	• Have no monks. • Have no shrines or relics. • Make the queen 'Supreme Governor' of the Church of England. • Punish those who refuse to accept the religious changes and who are a threat to the queen.

2 You have now gathered enough information to be able to answer the big question:
'Did England become Protestant in the sixteenth century?' **WS**
To do this, you will need to consider the following smaller questions. Jot down answers in note form in your book and then use them to help you with your answer to the big question.

- What religion was England in 1500? What did this mean to people?
- How did Henry VIII's actions change religion in England?
- How did England become more Protestant under Edward VI?
- How successful was Mary I in turning England back to Catholicism?
- What did Elizabeth I do to try to reach a settlement in religion?
- Was England more Protestant or more Catholic by the end of Elizabeth's reign?

Choose three new words you have learnt about religion in the sixteenth century. Write out definitions for each one. Test a friend on their meaning.

2

WHY WERE MARY I OF ENGLAND AND MARY, QUEEN OF SCOTS, SUCH CONTROVERSIAL FIGURES IN TUDOR ENGLAND?

WHY WERE PROTESTANTS BURNED AT THE STAKE DURING THE REIGN OF MARY I?

Objectives

In this section you will try to decide:
- why a Protestant was executed
- who was responsible for the execution.

You will analyse statements to reach a conclusion.

SOURCE A

A fictional TV detective.

Starter

- Who is the detective in Source A?
- What other famous detectives can you think of?
- Why are the detectives you have thought of successful at their job?

A historical mystery

You are now going to be a detective. The year is 1556. A man called Thomas Wilson has been executed by burning. Think back to what you learned about the religious changes in England.

💡 Why do you think he was executed?

💡 Who do you think was responsible for his death?

In groups, look at the statements below and then sort them to help you answer the questions that follow. Beware! There are some 'red herrings' – they are not relevant. **WS**

1 Thomas was born in 1515 during the reign of Henry VIII.

2 He supported the Reformation under Henry VIII, believing that the king was right to become Head of the Church of England.

3 Thomas made great changes to his church. He removed any signs of Catholicism including statues, pictures, the Latin service book and the statue of the Virgin Mary.

4 He was pleased when Edward VI became king in 1547 as Edward was a keen Protestant.

5 Mary banned the new English Prayer Book. Thomas continued to use it.

6 Edward VI was ill throughout his reign.

7 Mary declared the Pope as Head of the English Church and ordered everyone to worship as Catholics.

8 In 1549 Thomas enthusiastically introduced the new English Prayer Book.

9 In 1556 Thomas was arrested for using the English Prayer Book.

10 Under torture, Thomas refused to renounce his Protestant beliefs.

11 Elizabeth I was the younger daughter of Henry VIII.

12 Thomas was very upset when, in 1553, he heard of the death of Edward VI.

13 Mary, elder daughter of Henry VIII, became queen.

14 Mary died in 1558, lonely and unhappy.

15 There was a Catholic rebellion against Edward VI which was savagely crushed.

16 Thomas helped to translate the Bible into English in the early 1540s.

17 In 1538 Thomas decided on a career in the Church.

18 In 1542 Thomas became a priest in the English Protestant Church.

19 Thomas was alarmed because Queen Mary was a strict Catholic.

TASKS...

1 What were the:
   a) long-term
   b) short-term
   reasons for Thomas Wilson's execution?

2 **a)** Who was most responsible for his death?
   b) Which cards do you think are 'red herrings'?
   c) Compare your findings with other groups.

Plenary

Write a letter to Thomas Wilson's mother explaining why her son was executed and saying who you think was most responsible for his death.

Show your letter to someone else in your class. How different are the two letters?

DID MARY I DESERVE TO BE KNOWN AS 'BLOODY MARY'?

Objectives

In this section you will:
- examine evidence about the reign of Mary I
- decide how far you can trust the evidence
- make a judgement on whether Mary I deserved the nickname 'Bloody Mary'.

SOURCE A

O Lord, Receiue my spirite.

The burning of a Protestant, Thomas Hawkes, during the reign of Mary I. An illustration from Foxe's _Book of Martyrs_.

SOURCE B

Queen Mary believed that heretics – people who did not agree with the Catholic religion – had to be burned. The fire would be punishment but it would also burn away their sin. Two of the Protestants who were burned were Hugh Latimer and Nicholas Ridley. Latimer was a preacher who criticised rich people, as well as the Catholic religion. Ridley was the Bishop of London. However, the burnings did not turn people back to Catholicism and many of those who died became **martyrs**. People started to call the queen 'Bloody Mary'. When she died in 1558, people rejoiced.

An extract from a school textbook published in 1997.

Starter

What is happening in Source A? What questions would you ask about the event shown? Use the 5Ws – who, why, what, when and where – to help you frame your questions.

Mary I and the Protestants

Look at the evidence of Sources B to I and the map on page 30.

Key words

Martyr A person who is put to death for refusing to change their faith or beliefs.

💡 What other famous martyrs can you think of?

A Protestant woodcut from the 1560s, showing the deaths of Bishops Latimer and Ridley.

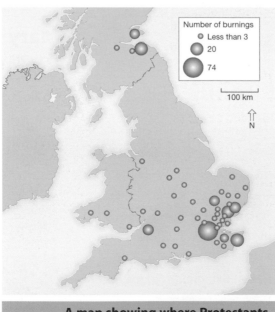

A map showing where Protestants were burned.

The whole number burned during the reign of Mary I was 284. There were burnt 5 bishops, 21 ministers, 8 gentlemen, 84 workers, 100 farmers, servants and labourers, 26 wives, 20 widows, 9 girls, 2 boys, 2 infants.

John Foxe, a Protestant minister, included these figures in his *Book of Martyrs*.

In 1554 Mary married Prince Philip, the son of the King of Spain. Spain was the most powerful country in Europe and it was also a very Catholic country. The English were worried that Philip would tell Mary how to run the country.

In 1554 there was a rebellion in Kent against the wedding. Soldiers were sent to stop the rebellion and its leaders were hanged. Many Protestants opposed Mary and between 1555 and 1558 over 8300 Protestants were killed.

An extract from a modern textbook.

SOURCE (F)

Thomas Cranmer, the Protestant Archbishop of Canterbury, was burned for not becoming a Catholic. An illustration from Foxe's *Book of Martyrs*.

SOURCE (G)

SOURCE (H)

A certain Rogers was burned publicly yesterday. Some of the onlookers wept, others prayed to God to give him strength to bear the pain, others gathered the ashes and the bones and wrapped them in paper to preserve them, others threatened the bishops. I think it would be wise not to be too firm against Protestants, otherwise I foresee that the people may cause a revolt. The lady Elizabeth has her supporters, and there are Englishmen who do not love foreigners.

Simon Renard, a Catholic, was the Spanish Ambassador in London. He wrote this letter to Philip of Spain after watching the first Protestant being burned at the stake in 1555.

Mary I blessing rings which were supposed to cure sickness. This picture was drawn by a Catholic in the sixteenth century.

SOURCE 1

We must be careful not to judge people in the past by our standards today. In the sixteenth century people were used to heretics being burned:

- Henry VII burned ten in 24 years.
- Henry VIII burned 81 in 38 years.
- Edward VI burned two in six years.
- Mary I burned 284 in five years.
- Elizabeth burned five in 45 years.
- Every year between 17 and 54 people were hanged in Essex for small-scale theft.
- After the Northern Rebellion in Elizabeth's reign, over 300 people were hanged.

An extract from a modern textbook.

TASKS...

1 Which sources suggest that Mary I deserved her nickname?
   Give reasons for each choice.

2 Which sources suggest that she did not?
   Give reasons for each choice.

3 From the evidence of the map and sources B to I, does Mary I deserve to be called 'Bloody Mary'? Give three reasons for your decision.

4 Imagine that Mary I is on her deathbed and decides to dictate her final letter to the people of England justifying her actions during her reign. Write out what you think she would say.
   Remember:
   - what the purpose of your letter is
   - you are the queen, writing to your subjects, so use a formal tone
   - to use evidence to support your actions
   - to write the letter in the first person.

Plenary

Write down one new word, or term, that you have learned in this chapter. Show it to someone else in the class. Ask them to give a definition of that term.

Now you could play a game of 'Taboo'. Think of a second term or word used in the chapter. Describe the word to your partner (without using the word itself!).

WHAT DO WE KNOW OF THE LIFE AND SCANDALS OF MARY, QUEEN OF SCOTS?

Objectives

In this section you will:
- examine aspects of Mary, Queen of Scots' controversial life and reign
- produce a lesson on Mary, Queen of Scots for younger pupils.

SOURCE Ⓐ

One evening in March 1566, Mary and her ladies-in-waiting were having supper with Rizzio. Suddenly the door burst open. Darnley and his followers pushed their way in. The women stood terrified. Rizzio clung pitifully to the Queen but Darnley's men dragged him away. Brutally they murdered him outside the door.

A description of the murder of Mary, Queen of Scots' secretary, Rizzio.

Starter

Imagine you are the first newspaper reporter at the scene of Rizzio's murder.

Write an eye-catching headline for the murder.

The key events and scandals of Mary, Queen of Scots' life

TASKS...

1 You will be reading about the key events and scandals in the life of Mary, Queen of Scots, and looking at source evidence. Once you have done this, in a group, prepare a lesson plan on the life and times of Mary, Queen of Scots, for year 5 pupils. Include the following:

> **Starter** Something to catch their attention and interest.
> **Activity** To get them researching and finding out.
> **Plenary** An interesting end to the lesson.
> **Follow-up** A task that they can carry out themselves.

Below are some hints and tips.
- Make the lesson as interesting and exciting as possible. You might want to make it a murder mystery, for example: did Mary, Queen of Scots, order the murder of Darnley? Why was she involved in two murders?
- What will you include? What will you leave out?
- Remember that you will have to simplify the information for younger students.

The information and Sources B–H below reveal the key events and scandals of Mary, Queen of Scots' life. Remember – your group has been asked to prepare a lesson on the life and times of Mary, Queen of Scots, for pupils in year 5.

SOURCE B

I know for certain that the Queen regrets her marriage. She hates the King (Darnley) and all his family. David Rizzio, with the consent of the King, will get his throat cut in the next ten days.

From a letter written by the English ambassador in Scotland three weeks before Rizzio's death.

In 1558 Mary, Queen of Scots, married Francis, the eldest son of the King of France. She became Queen of France as well as of Scotland. Soon afterwards her good fortune changed. When her husband died in 1561, she returned to Scotland. She was 19 years old.

Mary, Queen of Scots lived at Holyrood Palace in Edinburgh and, at first, seemed to rule well. She listened to the advice of her ministers and, although a Catholic, she tried not to offend leading Protestants. In 1565 she married a Scottish noble called Lord Darnley but it was not long before she realised that she had made a terrible mistake. Darnley was a coward and a drunkard and he was unable to help her rule Scotland.

SOURCE C

Mary, Queen of Scots began to rely on the advice of her private secretary. He was an Italian named David Rizzio. When Darnley realised that she preferred her secretary's company he planned to have him murdered.

Mary, Queen of Scots never forgave Darnley for Rizzio's murder.

A painting by William Allan of the murder of Rizzio in 1833.

SOURCE D

No more tears now. I will think about revenge.

Words spoken by Mary, Queen of Scots soon after Rizzio's murder.

SOURCE E

Darnley's death is planned. If I do not kill him, I cannot live in Scotland. He will destroy me.

John Hay's account of what the Earl of Bothwell said to him in 1566.

SOURCE F

After Rizzio's death Mary, Queen of Scots began to rely on the advice of another noble, the Earl of Bothwell. Then, a few months after Rizzio's murder, a mysterious explosion blew up Darnley's house. He must have been warned of the danger for he tried to escape, but as he ran into the garden he was murdered.

The chief suspect for the murder was the Earl of Bothwell. There were even rumours that Mary had helped to plan the murder. However, most people refused to believe that their queen would do such a thing! Then Mary, Queen of Scots, made a major mistake – she married the Earl of Bothwell. He was unpopular with both Protestants and Catholics and many people thought that he was responsible for Darnley's murder. Mary's close relationship with the Earl of Bothwell further damaged her reputation.

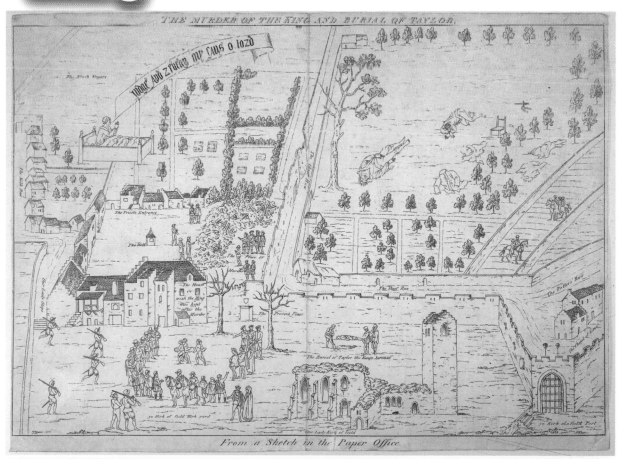

A sketch drawn at the time of Darnley's murder.

You and I are the most faithful couple that were ever united. Cursed be this fellow (Darnley) that troubles me so much.

From a letter which Mary, Queen of Scots was supposed to have written in 1567 to the Earl of Bothwell. Some historians think that it is a forgery.

Shocked by the rumours about Mary's involvement in Darnley's murder and by her marriage to the Earl of Bothwell, the Scots revolted against their queen. Two armies – the rebels and the supporters of Mary, Queen of Scots – met at Carberry Hill. However, the battle never began. When Mary saw how strong the opposing army was she sent Bothwell away and surrendered immediately. The leading lords made her a prisoner in Loch Leven Castle.

SOURCE H

A romantic painting of the battle of Carberry Hill in 1567.

Mary, Queen of Scots managed to escape. She was guided out of the castle by her 16-year-old page. No one heard them as they crept down to the shore. Swiftly, she was rowed across the loch to where friends were waiting to meet her. Mary raised a new army but it was defeated at the Battle of Langside. Mary then escaped and fled to England, where she asked her cousin, the Protestant Queen Elizabeth, to protect her.

Queen Elizabeth allowed Mary, Queen of Scots to remain in England. However, Elizabeth was worried that Mary might make a claim for the English throne, so for 19 years Elizabeth kept Mary prisoner in different castles. They included castles at Sheffield (where she stayed for 14 years), Bolton, Wakefield and Tutbury.

Plenary

Check your lesson plan. Have you missed out any important details?

WHAT SHOULD BE DONE ABOUT MARY, QUEEN OF SCOTS?

Objectives

In this section you will:
- look at the problems Elizabeth I faced in dealing with Mary, Queen of Scots.

You will try to decide the answers to these questions:
- Was Elizabeth I right to order the execution of Mary, Queen of Scots?
- Was Mary, Queen of Scots guilty of treason?

> Dear Agony Aunt
>
> I need your advice. I think my cousin is plotting to have me killed. What should I do?
>
> Elizabeth I

Starter

Jot down a quick reply to the 'Agony Aunt' letter. Share your reply with others in the class.

Now read the description of Mary's execution in Source A.

SOURCE A

Think of three key words to describe the execution. Share these with someone else in your class.

The prisoner took off her cloak as she moved towards the block. The crowd gazed at her bright scarlet dress and wondered whether she had worn this deliberately in defiance. She stepped forward, praying aloud in Latin as she knelt down. A woman gave her some dignity by placing a cloth over her face and pinning it in place. It took three blows of the axe to remove her head. After the first blow the prisoner could be heard to make no noise.

After the third fall of the axe the executioner grasped her wig to hold up the head for everyone to see. The crowd was shocked to see the grey hair of the prisoner as the head fell to the ground. After all, she was only 45 years old. A small, scared dog ran from underneath the skirts of the body, but it would not leave her. When news of the execution reached Elizabeth she was stunned. She screamed, shouted and demanded answers. She had not meant this to happen.

An account of Mary, Queen of Scots' execution from a modern textbook.

Was Mary guilty of treason? The evidence

As you read through the pieces of evidence against Mary, Queen of Scots, give each one a rating from 1 to 5 for how guilty each event shows Mary to be:

1 = Not Mary's idea and not involved – not guilty.

5 = Mary is totally involved – guilty.

SOURCE B

I cannot but praise your desire to hinder the plans of our enemies who seek to destroy our religion in this realm. Long ago I pointed out to other foreign Catholic princes that the longer we delayed intervening in England, the greater the advantage of our opponents. Meanwhile the Catholics here, exposed to all kinds of cruelty, steadily grow less in numbers and power. Everything being prepared, and the forces being ready, I must in some way be got from here to await foreign assistance.

Mary, Queen of Scots' letter to Babington. It was written in code but Walsingham had it deciphered.

The Babington Plot, 1586

Babington and other Catholics planned to kill Queen Elizabeth and put Mary, Queen of Scots on the throne. Babington wrote to Mary, Queen of Scots who replied, in code, agreeing to the plot. The letters were hidden in beer barrels and smuggled in and out of the castle. Elizabeth's spies cracked the code and Elizabeth now had the evidence she needed to prove that Mary, Queen of Scots was plotting to execute her.

The Throckmorton Plot, 1583

Throckmorton was a Catholic who took letters from Mary, Queen of Scots to the Spanish Ambassador. There was a plot by English Catholics to rebel with help from Spain. Again, Elizabeth's spies found out. Throckmorton and others were executed.

Philip of Spain

Mary, Queen of Scots was a Catholic. The King of Spain, Philip, was also a Catholic. He had been married to Mary I, the Catholic Queen of England. Queen Elizabeth was a Protestant and so England's relations with Spain grew tense in the 1580s. Many Catholics in Spain thought that Mary, Queen of Scots should replace Elizabeth because England needed a Catholic queen. Elizabeth could not be sure that Mary, Queen of Scots would not seek help from Philip and Catholic Spain for her cause.

The Ridolfi Plot, 1571

This was a plot to overthrow Elizabeth. The plotters intended to marry Mary, Queen of Scots to the Duke of Norfolk, the leading Catholic English noble, and then place her on the throne. The plotters were to be helped by the Pope and the King of Spain. Elizabeth's spies found out about the plot and the Duke of Norfolk was executed. There was no evidence that Mary herself had been involved in this plot.

SOURCE C

Sir Francis Walsingham.

Sir Francis Walsingham

He was the head of Elizabeth's secret service. He had more than 70 spies in towns and ports throughout Europe. These spies sent him news of Catholic plots against Elizabeth. His spies found the letter that Mary, Queen of Scots wrote to Babington. Some historians claim that Walsingham was out to get Mary, Queen of Scots and could have made up the evidence.

The Northern Rebellion, 1569

Although the main religion in England was Protestant, many people in the north of England remained Catholic at heart. Also, the nobles there wanted more power for themselves. Because Mary, Queen of Scots was Catholic, they planned to seize her from prison and march to London. There they would force Elizabeth to dismiss her Protestant advisers and restore the Catholic religion. When Elizabeth heard about this plot she sent her troops north. They defeated the rebels easily and hanged 800 of them.

TASKS...

1 Do you think Mary Queen of Scots was guilty of treason?

   a) Find three reasons to prove her guilt. Share your reasons with someone else in the class. Do they have the same reasons?

   b) Is there any evidence to prove Mary was not guilty? Share your answer with someone else in the class. Do they have the same evidence?

2 What should Elizabeth do? Below are her choices:

> **Choice 1:**
> Hand Mary back to the Scots who might well put her to death for murder. Elizabeth is horrified at the thought of people executing their own queen, and her cousin. It would reflect badly on Elizabeth too.

> **Choice 3:**
> Keep Mary permanently captive. This will avoid Elizabeth having to kill her cousin but will leave Mary at the centre of plots to overthrow Elizabeth.

> **Choice 2:**
> Allow Mary to be free in England. Mary might attract friends, especially Catholic nobles who do not like Elizabeth, and lead a revolt against her. After all, Mary is attractive and lively and has already had three husbands.

> **Choice 4:**
> Execute Mary. Elizabeth has clear evidence that Mary has taken part in Babington's plan to murder her. She could set up a court to try Mary and, if she is guilty, have her executed. However, this means that she has to order the death of her own cousin and a fellow monarch.

   a) In groups, using the table below, do a SWOT analysis on each of Elizabeth's choices. Report back to the rest of the class with your decisions. **WS**

   b) What is your final decision? Give reasons for your decision.

Strengths	Weaknesses	Opportunities	Threats

   c) Write a diary entry for Queen Elizabeth for 3 February 1587 in which she explains:
   - the choices she had
   - her difficulties in making the decision
   - what she finally decided and why.

The execution of Mary, Queen of Scots, drawn by an eyewitness. Servants are shown outside burning her clothes.

Plenary

Elizabeth decided to have Mary, Queen of Scots, executed in 1587. Did she make the right choice?

Now that you have read the evidence, write a detailed reply to the Agony Aunt letter which you read on page 38. Compare answers with someone else in your class.

WHY WERE ENGLISH PEOPLE FIGHTING EACH OTHER IN THE SEVENTEENTH CENTURY?

WHO OR WHAT CAUSED THE CIVIL WAR?

Objectives

In this section you will try to understand:
- who or what caused the Civil War. Was it Charles I, Parliament or were there other reasons?
- who or what was most to blame for the Civil War.

Starter

Civil War breaks out in England after series of clashes between Queen and Prime Minister!

The Prime Minister, Archibald Knowitall, finally lost patience with Queen Gertrude when she stopped his attempts to ban smoking in public places. The PM insists that the Queen has ignored hundreds of years of history and has taken the powers of her Prime Minister. The Queen, for her part, insists that she still has the power to stop laws which she believes are against the interests of her people. Neither Queen Gertrude nor the PM will allow the other to have the final say on this matter.

This sort of situation is unlikely to happen today, but if it did, which side would you support and why? Does the person sitting next to you share your views?

Why is a clash between the Queen and the Prime Minister unlikely to lead to Civil War today?

What happened during the Civil War?

During the Civil War, the people of England were divided. Supporters of King Charles I – Royalists, or **Cavaliers** as they were known – fought against the supporters of Parliament, known as Parliamentarians or **Roundheads**, led by Oliver Cromwell. Many families were divided by the Civil War. Fathers, mothers, sons and daughters supported different sides.

The Civil War lasted from 1642 to 1649 and brought victory to Parliament. In 1649 Charles I was put on trial by Parliament, found guilty of **treason** and executed.

From 1649 until 1660, England, for the only time in its history, was not ruled by a monarch but as a republic. This republic was controlled by Oliver Cromwell until his death in 1658. In 1660, the **monarchy** was restored under Charles II. Events had turned full circle.

Key words

Cavaliers and Roundheads
The nicknames of the two sides came from insults they gave each other. Supporters of Parliament said the Royalists were like brutal Spanish horse-soldiers called cavaliers. In 1642, London apprentices with short hair had rioted against Charles, so their opponents called them Roundheads.

Treason Betraying your country.

Monarchy When a monarch, such as a king, queen, emperor or empress rules a country.

What happened in the years before the Civil War?

In the years before the Civil War there were economic, social and political changes which eventually brought conflict between the king and Parliament. A growing and powerful middle class had emerged who wanted more of a say in how the country was run. At the same time, the position and powers of the monarchy had increased under Tudor rulers such as Henry VIII and Elizabeth I.

There were also long-term religious changes. Many strict Protestants, known as **Puritans**, had become MPs by the time Charles I became king in 1625. They wanted religion to be simple and hated priests and bishops. They also demanded a greater say in how the country was run and less power for the king.

TASKS...

1 Read pages 44–8 and Sources A–G.

2 After you have read *each* one, make a timeline by jotting down any relevant dates and the important things that happened.

Key words

Puritans Strict Protestants who wanted plain and simple church services. They tried to be more 'pure' in their religious practices.

Charles I strongly believed in the 'Divine Right of Kings'. He thought that monarchs received their power and right to rule from God and that they therefore must be obeyed. Charles I shared these beliefs with his father, James I.

💡 What reasons can you see so far for conflict between Charles I and Parliament?

The reign of Charles I

Charles I's reign started badly. In 1625 he married Henrietta Maria, the sister of the King of France. She was a Catholic, and members of Parliament (MPs) were alarmed because they feared that she might make Charles and any royal children Catholic too.

SOURCE A

Charles I with the symbols of royal power – the crown, orb and sceptre.

Parliament and the Petition of Right

Early in Charles's reign, England became involved in expensive foreign wars – with the Austrian Empire in 1625 and against France two years later. This meant that Charles was very short of money and so he forced rich people to lend him money. Then, in 1628, Charles asked Parliament to allow him to raise **customs duties** on wines and many other goods. MPs, shocked by these forced loans and foreign wars, presented Charles with the Petition of Right (see Source B on page 46).

Key words

Customs duties Taxes that are added to the price of goods which are imported into a country.

SOURCE B

It is declared by a law of King Edward I that there should be no taxes without the agreement of Parliament. In the reign of King Edward III it was declared that no person should be forced to make any loans to the king against his will. Yet recently, some people have been asked to lend money to your Majesty. When they have refused they have been ordered to appear before the Privy Council and some of them have been imprisoned against the laws of the country.

An extract from the Petition of Right, written in 1628.

Key words

Presbyterian Protestants who believe that the Church should be run by people of equal rank or status.

Parliament asked the king for an end to forced loans and imprisonment without trial. At first, Charles agreed. However, when Parliament granted him an increase in customs duties in 1629 but for one year only, Charles believed this to be an attack on his freedom to rule. He dismissed Parliament and went on to rule for 11 years without Parliament. This time is referred to as the period of 'personal rule'. Charles's enemies called it the '11 Years Tyranny'.

Religious changes

In 1633 Charles made William Laud Archbishop of Canterbury. Laud was a Protestant but he did not like Puritans and thought they had too much influence on the Church of England. He therefore made several changes which returned church services to a more Catholic style of worship. He brought back stained-glass windows, a railed-off altar at the east end of the church and special clothes for priests. Many Puritans were furious, believing that Laud was making the Church of England too much like the Catholic Church.

In 1637 Charles tried to force religious change on the people of Scotland where most people followed the **Presbyterian** religion. Charles wanted the Scottish Protestants to accept the new English Prayer Book. However, the Scottish Presbyterians thought that the prayer book reflected a more Catholic style worship, which they refused to accept. In St Giles' Cathedral in Edinburgh rioting took place on the first Sunday that the English Prayer Book was used (see Source C).

SOURCE C

The Arch-Prelate of St Andrewes in Scotland reading the new Service-booke in his pontificalibus assaulted by men & Women, with Crickets stooles Stickes and Stones.

A seventeenth-century engraving showing rioting in Scotland against the English Prayer Book in 1637.

Presbyterians throughout Scotland refused to accept the English Prayer Book, so in 1639 King Charles sent an army to force the Scots to accept it. However, the English army was no match for the well-trained Scots army, and was defeated.

Charles had no money to raise a second army to send to Scotland. In despair, he recalled Parliament in 1639 and asked for a **grant**. Parliament refused, so Charles dismissed Parliament again. It had been in session for less than a month, so it became known as the Short Parliament.

Charles took the money he needed to raise a second army, but this was also defeated by the Scots, and the king was forced to sign the Treaty of Ripon in 1640. By this treaty, Charles handed over control of six northern counties of England and agreed to pay the Scots £850 a day.

SOURCE D

I shall explain to you the grievances which trouble the country … Firstly, Parliament was dissolved before our complaints were heard. Several gentlemen were imprisoned for speaking freely to Parliament.
Secondly, there have been changes in matters of religion. The introduction of Catholic ceremonies, of altars, bowing towards the east, pictures, crucifixes, crosses and the like.
Thirdly, there is an attack on our property. The taking of taxes, without any grant or law.

Part of a speech made by John Pym, a leading MP, in April 1640.

Later that year Charles was forced to recall Parliament again in order to raise money. This was known as the Long Parliament – because of the length of time it lasted, from 1640 to 1653. This time Parliament was determined to reduce the powers of the king.

Key words

Grant A gift of money that requires official approval.

Rebellion in Ireland

In 1641 there was rebellion in Ireland because Irish Catholics feared that the English Parliament would try to pass anti-Catholic laws. Catholics led by Phelim O'Neill attacked towns and killed 3000 Protestants in Ulster (see Source E). Charles needed more money to put down this rebellion and an army to defeat the Irish rebels. However, the MPs, led by John Pym, a strict Puritan, insisted that they should decide who led this army. The king refused to let Parliament decide.

Driuinge Men Women & children by hund: reds vpon Briges & casting them into Riuers, who drowned not were killed with poles & shot with muskets.

A contemporary drawing, published in England, showing Irish Catholics killing Protestant settlers in Ulster in 1641.

Parliament opposes the king

Parliament now forced Charles to make some changes. MPs demanded that the king get rid of his Chief Minister, the Earl of Strafford, and Archbishop Laud. Both Strafford and Laud were hated for carrying out the wishes of Charles I. Strafford, a close friend of the king, was executed in 1641. Archbishop Laud was imprisoned and in 1645 he was executed. The MPs also abolished some unpopular taxes and closed down Star Chamber, the court that had been used to punish Charles's enemies.

In November 1641 Pym put before Parliament a long list of what the king had done wrong during his reign. This was known as the Grand Remonstrance. It condemned ministers chosen by the king and insisted that they should be chosen by Parliament. After long debate the Remonstrance was put to the vote and approved. Charles was furious and was determined to show who ruled the country. On 4 January 1642, he went to Westminster with 400 soldiers to arrest Pym and four other rebel MPs. However, the five MPs were warned in advance and managed to escape by boat down the River Thames.

Many people were shocked by Charles's actions. By law, MPs could not be arrested when they were in the House of Commons.

This was painted in the nineteenth century for the House of Commons.
It shows the five MPs escaping by boat.

Tuesday, 4 January 1642.
The five gentlemen which were to be accused came into the House, and there was information that they should be taken by force. A little after, the king came with all his guard. He told us he would not break our privileges but treason had no privilege.

He asked the Speaker if the five were present. The Speaker fell on his knees and said he had neither eyes, nor tongue, to see or say anything but what the MPs commanded him. Then the king told him he thought his own eyes were good and then said, his birds were flown.

An account by an MP, Sir Ralph Verney, who was present when the king entered the Commons.

TASKS...

Work in groups.

1 Use three different coloured highlighter pens to show those events on your timeline (page 44) for which you think Charles was to blame, those for which you feel Parliament was to blame and those involving other factors. Make a key to explain what each colour signifies.

2 Make a copy of the table below in your books. Use information from your timeline to complete the table.

Who or what was responsible for the outbreak of Civil War?		
The King	*Parliament*	*Other Factors*

3 Draw a line, like the one below, and decide where you would put Charles I, Parliament and each of the other factors.

●————————————————————————————————————●

To blame   Not to blame

4 Now compare this to the conclusions reached by other groups in your class.
   a) How different are they?
   b) Why are they different?
   c) Did anyone sympathise with Charles?

5 On your own, summarise who or what caused the Civil War. You could:
   • write a summary of less than 100 words
   • do a storyboard
   • draw a picture or a mind map.

Plenary

Discuss in your group how you came to your conclusions about who or what caused the Civil War.

WHY WAS KING CHARLES I DEFEATED?

Objectives

In this section you will:
- work out reasons for the defeat of Charles I
- decide on the importance of each reason.

SOURCE A

Parliamentarian propaganda of 1644, showing the murder of women and children by Royalist forces.

Starter

What are Sources A and B trying to show about the other side in the Civil War? Why are they showing this?

Sources A and B are examples of propaganda. Propaganda is often used in war. Source C is an example of propaganda used during the First World War by America against Germany.

SOURCE B

Title page from Mercurius Rusticus, the Royalist newspaper. It shows attacks carried out by Parliamentarians.

SOURCE C

'The beastly Hun' – an American propaganda poster used in the First World War. The 'mad brute' is Germany.

How *do you think propaganda might be used? Tell your ideas to a partner and see what they think.*

Why do both sides in a war use propaganda?

TIMELINE OF THE CIVIL WAR 1642–9

1642 Battle of Edgehill ends in a stalemate.

1643 Royalist army fails to reach London.
Royalist army captures Bristol.
Cromwell trains his New Model Army.

1644 The Scots join the Civil War on Parliament's side. The Parliamentarians defeat Prince Rupert and the Royalists at the Battle of Marston Moor.

1645 New Model Army fights on Parliament's side.
The Roundheads defeat Prince Rupert and the Royalists at the Battle of Naseby.

1646 Parliament captures Oxford from Charles I.

1648 Cromwell defeats Charles.

1649 Charles is arrested and put on trial.

The Civil War, 1642–9

As you read through the account in this section, you might find it helpful to jot down the reasons for Charles's defeat using a spider diagram or mind map.

Oliver Cromwell and the New Model Army

Oliver Cromwell was an MP and a Puritan. He had been furious with Charles I's refusal to give into Parliament's demands (see pages 48-9). He decided to form an army to fight the king's forces. Before this time no national army existed. Instead, local nobles and some cities organised and paid for their own troops. Cromwell showed a great talent for warfare and, between 1644 and 1645, set up an army known as the New Model Army. Cromwell picked only men who were committed to Parliament's cause and trained and disciplined them thoroughly. For example, the army's horses were trained to advance at a trot, which was much easier to control than the usual cavalry charge.

Cromwell took great care of his soldiers and made sure that they were paid well. In return, they were expected to behave well and not to swear or become drunk. The soldiers were also religious men, believing they were doing God's will.

A modern artist's impression of the New Model Army.

Key battles of the Civil War

Battle of Edgehill, October 1642

This was the first major battle of the Civil War. The king's nephew, Prince Rupert, commanded the Royalist cavalry. He was young and inexperienced. The Royalists attacked the Parliamentarian forces and each side fought until exhausted. The battle ended in a **stalemate** but it stopped Charles from capturing London, the key city for controlling finance and communications.

Battle of Marston Moor, July 1644

Prince Rupert faced the Parliamentarians at Marston Moor, near York, on 2 July. He made the mistake of believing that the enemy forces were not ready and that there would be no fighting on that day. Indeed, he was starting to eat his supper when the Parliamentarians attacked. The Royalist cavalry were scattered and, although the Royalist **infantry** fought bravely, they were eventually defeated. The king lost the north of England to Parliamentary forces.

Key words

Stalemate A conflict in which neither side is the winner.
Infantry Soldiers who fight on foot.

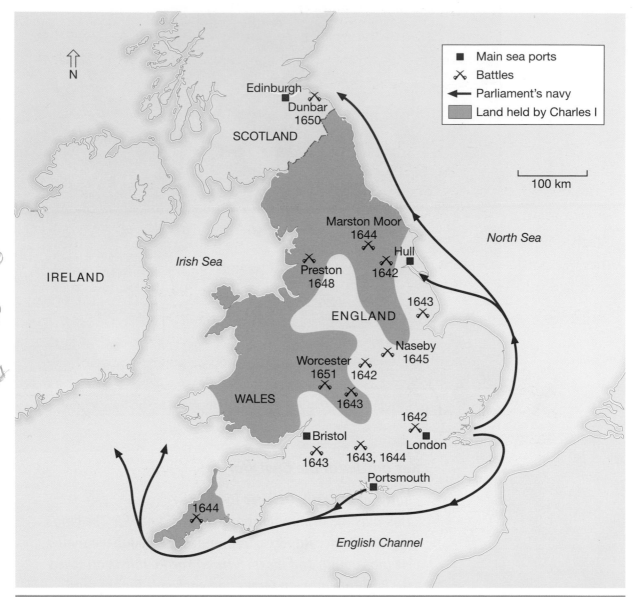

Main sea ports
Battles
Parliament's navy
Land held by Charles I

N

SCOTLAND

Edinburgh
Dunbar
1650

100 km

North Sea

Marston Moor
1644

Hull
1642

Irish Sea

IRELAND

Preston
1648

1643

ENGLAND

Naseby
1645

Worcester
1651

1642

WALES

1643

1642

Bristol

1643

1643, 1644

London

Portsmouth

1644

English Channel

The key battles of the Civil War and land held by King Charles and Parliament.

Battle of Naseby, June 1645

This was the first battle in which Royalist troops faced the New Model Army. The cavalry, led by Prince Rupert, attacked but his men charged too quickly and too far. Cromwell's horsemen defeated the cavalry before the prince could arrive. This was the last major battle of the war. The king and his forces were defeated.

Why was Charles I defeated?

Charles made several mistakes during the Civil War, while Parliament had many strengths. The statements below are a mixture of Charles's mistakes and Parliament's strengths.

The king had rich supporters but they ran out of money. Most gentlemen in the areas he controlled refused to give him any money. His soldiers at the Battle of Naseby were badly equipped compared to those of Parliament. After this battle Charles might have recruited another army but he had no money to pay the soldiers.

Parliament controlled the south east of England, the richest part of the country, and this meant that it was able to finance the war. The MP, John Pym, had set up a well-organised system to supply Parliament's army with money.

Parliament chose very good commanders including Oliver Cromwell and Sir Thomas Fairfax. Fairfax had been a soldier before the Civil War and everyone on the parliamentary side respected him.

Charles placed Prince Rupert, who was young and inexperienced, in command of his armies.

The navy supported Parliament which made it much easier to get men and supplies from abroad.

Charles left London at the very start of the Civil War, which meant that Parliament controlled the capital with all its resources and communications, and strategic position. In 1643, Charles tried unsuccessfully to capture London.

Parliament gained the support of the Scots by promising that it would set up a Presbyterian Church in England like the one in Scotland. In return, an army of 20,000 Scots invaded England and joined with the Parliamentarians to defeat the Royalists at the Battle of Marston Moor.

TASKS...

1 Why was Charles I defeated? Work in groups to find out the reasons for Charles I's defeat in the Civil War.

  a) Try to organise your reasons under various headings, for example 'Parliament's strengths'.

  b) How important was each reason? Put a rating of 1–5 next to each reason where 1 = unimportant; 5 = very important.

2 On a sheet of A3 paper make a concept map showing the reasons for Charles's defeat. Below is an example of a concept map showing the causes of the Civil War, to help you.

3 Now, on your own, write an answer to the following question:
Why was Charles I defeated in the Civil War?
WS

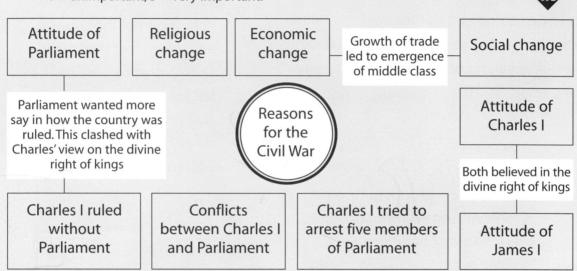

| Attitude of Parliament | Religious change | Economic change | Growth of trade led to emergence of middle class | Social change |

Parliament wanted more say in how the country was ruled. This clashed with Charles' view on the divine right of kings

Reasons for the Civil War

Attitude of Charles I

Both believed in the divine right of kings

| Charles I ruled without Parliament | Conflicts between Charles I and Parliament | Charles I tried to arrest five members of Parliament | Attitude of James I |

Plenary

In groups, read the following account of the Civil War and see how many inaccuracies you can find. **WS**

An account of the English Civil War by Professor Botchit

The Civil War broke out in 1643, with the first battle at Edgehill where the New Model Army fought against the Royalists led by Prince Rupert. The battle was a stalemate but prevented Parliament from capturing London.

Two years later, the two armies met at Marston Moor in the south-west. This time the Royalists were victorious because of a fast attack by the cavalry led by Prince Rupert.

York was now safe. The final major battle was at Naseby in 1847. The Royalists were defeated and Charles had lost the war.

Parliament persuaded the Irish to fight on their side and Charles won the support of the Scots. Parliament was victorious because Richard Cromwell had set up the New Model Army before the war even started. They also had a popular commander called George Fairfax.

Once you have spotted all the inaccuracies, write out the account with all the mistakes corrected.

WAS CHARLES I A TRAITOR?

In this section, through role play and by investigating sources, you will be able to:
- Make a judgement on Charles I – was he a traitor or not?
- Decide whether he should have been executed.

Starter

Write out five questions that you would like to ask about the events in Source A. As you work through this section see if you can answer these questions.

The execution of Charles I in 1649, painted at the time.

The trial and execution of Charles I

In 1649 Charles I was arrested and put on trial in a special court set up by Parliament in Westminster Hall. He was accused of trying to rule as a **tyrant** and of causing the misery and bloodshed that occurred in the Civil War.

There were supposed to be 135 people acting as judges but only 85 turned up. Many MPs thought that the king should be returned to power. Some MPs disagreed with the trial and many were frightened by the thought of executing the king.

- Name a present-day tyrant.

- Why do you think this person is a tyrant?

SOURCE B

Truly I desire people's liberty and freedom as much as anybody … but I must tell you that their liberty and freedom consists in having a government and laws. It is not having a share in government … that is nothing to do with them. A subject and a sovereign are clear different things … If I would have given way … I need not have come here … I am a martyr of the people …

Charles I's last speech.

SOURCE C

As far as the soldiers were concerned, Charles' defeats in battle were a sign that God was against him. Furthermore, he was a traitor to have plotted with the Scots and invited them into England.

An extract from a history textbook published in 1992.

Although Charles I was a shy man who normally stammered, he talked confidently at his trial. He refused to answer the charges made against him and insisted that the court was not a proper court and did not have the power to try him. However, this did not stop 59 of the 85 judges finding Charles guilty, and he was sentenced as follows:

'The said Charles Stuart, as a Tyrant, Traitor and Murderer and public enemy to be put to death by the severing of his head from his body.'

Charles was executed on 30 January 1649 on a scaffold set up in Whitehall, London. He made a short speech and then laid his head on the block. There was said to have been a great groan from the watching crowd as his head was cut off.

Now look at the following evidence relating to the trial and execution of Charles I.

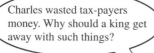

Charles is a tyrant. He rules according to his will rather than the law.

Life won't be the same if the king is gone. I know most people are against the execution.

Charles wasted tax-payers money. Why should a king get away with such things?

If Charles is executed it will be the army's doing, not the people's.

Charles tried to take away the freedom of the people. He has to be stopped.

Parliament promises peace in England. I say end the wars that Charles started!

No-one has the right to deny the divine right of kings.

A cartoon showing contemporary arguments for and against the execution of Charles I.

SOURCE D

Charles Stuart, King of England, trusted to govern according to the laws of the land, had a wicked design to create for himself an unlimited power to rule according to his will and to overthrow the rights and liberties of the people. To do this he treacherously waged a war against Parliament and the people. He is thus responsible for all the treasons, murders, rapings, burnings, damage and desolation, caused by the wars. He is therefore a TYRANT, traitor and murderer.

The charges against Charles I at his trial.

SOURCE E

The trial of Charles I in Westminster Hall, London, 1649.

TASKS...

1 Look at Source B.
   a) Why does Charles believe he is a 'martyr of the people'?
   b) Have your views of Charles changed as a result of reading his last speech?

2 Look at the cartoon on page 58 and Sources C and D.
   a) What arguments are presented against Charles?
   b) Do you think the charges made against Charles in Source D are fair?

3 It is the trial of Charles I. Use the evidence to prepare speeches for the trial using persuasive language. Imagine you are *either*:
   - Charles's lawyer (the defence lawyer). Sources A and B should be especially useful. Charles will be trying to prove that he is not a traitor and should not be executed ... OR
   - Parliament's lawyer (the prosecution). Sources B, C and D should be useful. Parliament will be trying to provide evidence of the king's guilt and justify his execution.
   Try to anticipate what the opposing lawyer will say.

Plenary

Do you think Parliament had the right to kill the king? Was there an alternative?

Could you imagine this happening in Britain today? Explain why.

HOW MUCH DID ENGLAND CHANGE AS A RESULT OF THE CIVIL WAR?

Objectives

In this section you will look at change and **continuity**, and a variety of sources, so you can decide:

- how much change there was in England in the period from the execution of Charles I in 1649 to the restoration of his son, Charles II, as king in 1660
- how much things stayed the same
- what role Cromwell played
- why there are so many different interpretations of Cromwell.

Key words

Continuity Things staying the same or hardly changing.

Starter

Sir Hugo Ponsonby-Smythe was a Royalist. Some of the events described below would have pleased him, others would have made him unhappy.

1 In 1642 Charles I stormed into Parliament to arrest five MPs. All five managed to escape.

2 The Royalist army was defeated at the Battle of Marston Moor in 1644.

3 In 1644 the Royalists were able to hold off attacks by Parliament's forces in the south and west.

4 Charles persuaded the Irish Catholics to fight on his side.

5 In 1645 the Royalist army was defeated at the Battle of Naseby.

6 In 1647 Charles was imprisoned in Carisbrooke Castle.

7 In 1648 Charles escaped from Carisbrooke Castle. In secret he arranged for another army to march into England on his side.

8 In 1649 Charles was put on trial and found guilty of treason.

10 In his last speech Charles said he was 'a martyr of the people'.

9 In 1649 Charles was beheaded.

Plot Sir Hugo's reactions to events on a living graph like the one below. Compare your living graph with others in your class. What are the similarities? Are there any differences? If so, why? **WS**

TASKS...

1 As you read through the information below, draw two spider diagrams in your books or on a large piece of paper:

   • one showing change in the period 1649–60

   • one showing continuity in the same period.

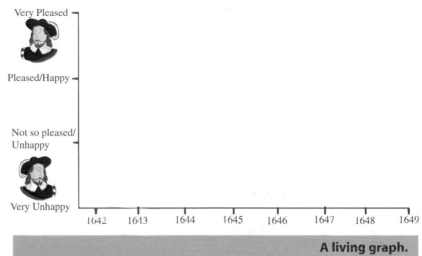

A living graph.

What happened between 1649 and 1660?

Quarrels in Parliament

There were many quarrels between Parliament and the army generals between 1649 and 1653. Having rid the country of the king, the MPs were unable to fulfil the high hopes for a better England. A council made up of leading MPs was responsible for running the country but the council couldn't agree on decisions. In 1653 Cromwell lost patience and turned out the MPs by force – this marked the end of the Long Parliament.

The army leaders tried for six years to find a new system of ruling the country. They made Cromwell Lord Protector, giving him the power to rule England for life in the place of a king. Cromwell did call some parliaments, but none of them pleased him, so he kept all the power to himself.

Problems in Ireland

In 1649, Cromwell went to Ireland to crush a Catholic rebellion. He destroyed the Drogheda **garrison** and massacred 3500 people. He treated Irish Catholics at Wexford in the same way. His treatment of the Irish was very harsh in order to prevent any future rebellions.

The Levellers

At Burford, in May 1649, Cromwell captured 340 **Levellers** in a night attack. The Levellers were a group that wanted to change the way the country was governed.

Key words

Garrison A military camp where troops are stationed.
Levellers Puritans who thought that all men were equal and should share power.

This made the Levellers a dangerous threat to Cromwell. He locked them up in a church and forced them to watch as three Leveller soldiers were shot dead by firing squad. (You will read more about the Levellers on pages 73–6.)

Foreign wars

During this period Cromwell also led England to war with the Dutch (1652–4) and then, in 1655, with Spain. England was successful in both wars.

Puritan ideals

Cromwell's government saw itself as protector of the Puritans so people had to live a Puritan lifestyle. No swearing, gambling or drunkenness was allowed. Sport was banned, including football – anyone caught playing could be whipped. Theatres were closed and the celebration of Christmas was banned. Although everyone had to live by Puritan ideals, they did not have to become Puritans and people in England were not persecuted for their religion.

Under Cromwell taxes on the rich increased and the money was given to the poor. The poor were treated better during this period.

The press was **censored**. This meant that newspapers could only print what Cromwell allowed them to print.

Cromwell died in 1658 and for a short time his son, Richard, ruled as Lord Protector. However, Richard was not a strong leader like his father and resigned in 1659. The following year the son of Charles I was restored to the throne and made King Charles II.

Key words

Censored Checked by the authorities and altered to suit them.

TASKS...

1 **a)** On each of your spider diagrams, shade each of the four following factors in different colours:
   - political
   - religious
   - social
   - policies abroad.

   b) Which factor experienced the most change?

   c) Which factor experienced the least change?

2 Think about the changes which took place in England from 1649 until 1660. Were those changes good or bad for England? Explain your answer.

3 Explain if you think Oliver Cromwell was a better ruler than:
   a) Charles I
   b) Henry VIII.

Different interpretations of Cromwell

Oliver Cromwell's remains were dug up three years after his death and his body was publicly beheaded.

Look at Source A.

💡 Why do you think that there is a spike through Cromwell's skull?

💡 Who do you think did this and when?

💡 What does this tell you about attitudes to Cromwell?

💡 Can you remember what happened to other 'traitors' before Cromwell? For example, think back to the leaders of the Peasants' Revolt.

There have been many different interpretations of Oliver Cromwell, both at the time and from later historians.

💡 As you read Sources B–E think about which sources are:

- sympathetic to Cromwell
- against him
- neither.

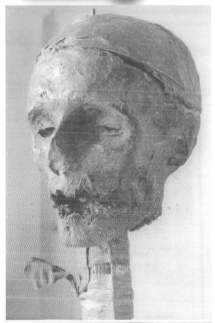

Cromwell's skull on a spike.

He is so wicked that he is damned, for which hell-fire is prepared, yet he had some qualities which have caused the memory of some men in all ages to be celebrated; and he will be looked upon by people in years to come as a brave bad man.

Lord Clarendon, who supported Charles I and became chief minister under Charles II in the 1660s.

You … the author of liberty … have outstripped not only the achievements of our kings, but even the legends of our heroes … You have taken upon yourself … to rule three powerful nations … to lead their peoples to a better standard of morality and discipline.

John Milton, a writer and poet, who served in the government of Cromwell.

Oliver Cromwell died hated by all except a few close friends. It is only in the last hundred years that he has been given the honour due to him in English history. He was successful in his wars abroad and was able to defeat the rebellion in Ireland. At home he gave the English people both peace and order after long years of trouble.

A historian writing in 1952.

In the nineteenth century as England moved towards democracy and Parliament became more important in helping rule the country, historians became more sympathetic towards Cromwell. Yet here was the man who ruthlessly crushed rebellion in Ireland, supported the execution of Charles I, ordered the shooting of the leading Levellers and, above all else, banned football and Christmas.

An extract from a history textbook written in 1996.

TASKS...

1 Make a copy of the table below in your book.

Source	Sympathetic to Cromwell	Opposed to Cromwell	Neither	Reason for interpretation
A				
B				
C				
D				
E				

a) For the first three columns give a brief explanation for your choice. You could, for example, pick out certain words or facts mentioned in the source.

b) In the final column try to give at least one reason for the interpretation. This could be:

- The bias of the person writing it – did the author like or dislike Cromwell?
- The achievements or events in Cromwell's career which the writer has highlighted.

2 Write your own interpretation of Cromwell. Construct your answer so that it has

- an introduction
- an interpretation
- a conclusion.

This could be done in the form of an obituary. Remember to use suitable language in your obituary. You might want to find examples of obituaries in newspapers to help you write your own one for Oliver Cromwell. What sort of tone does an obituary have? Why do you think this is?

Plenary

Imagine Oliver Cromwell was alive today. You might like to ask him some questions.

Pretend you are going to do a TV interview. Write a list of questions you would ask Oliver Cromwell. What answers would he give?

HOW FAR DID THE PURITANS CHANGE LIFE IN ENGLAND IN THE LATE 1640s AND EARLY 1650s?

WHAT DID IT MEAN TO BE A PURITAN?

Objectives

By the end of this section you will:
- know that Puritans wanted people to live 'godly' lives
- understand what activities were considered 'godly' and 'ungodly'
- be able to question sources to follow a line of enquiry.

Starter

From your previous work on religion, try to remember two things which made Protestants different from Catholics. Exchange your ideas with someone else in your class and try to remember theirs as well as yours. If their ideas are the same, try to think of a different idea to add to your list. Then exchange all the ideas you have with another member of the class. Do this until you have ten different things which show the differences between Catholics and Protestants.

Why did attitudes towards religion change after the Civil War?

In the years between the execution of King Charles I in 1649 and the death of Oliver Cromwell in 1658 some dramatic changes took place in the lives of the people of England.

At the end of the Civil War in 1649 the supporters of Parliament had killed the king. They needed to put something in place of the monarchy to run the country and this led to a period of uncertainty. However, Charles I had not just been the leader of the government, he had also been the Head of the Church of England. His insistence on making everyone conform to his view of religion had been one of the major causes of the Civil War.

Now that Charles I was dead the people who had opposed him tried to impose their religious views on the country. For a while a few Puritans in the House of Commons governed the country. They controlled religious belief in England and they also made many changes to people's way of life.

What did Puritans believe?

The Puritans were strict Protestants who thought that the Church of England was too like the Catholic Church. They wanted a religion that was purer and simpler and which did not need bishops to run it. They believed in a disciplined life of worship and showed their serious approach to religion through their attention to Bible reading and prayer, their simple dress and their efforts to lead a 'godly' life – a life 'free of sin'.

💡 If you wanted to make people follow more 'godly' lives, what things would you change? For example, would you stop all gambling?

If so, from where would the charities that receive donations from the National Lottery get their funding?

TASKS...

1 In pairs, brainstorm what you think a 'godly' life or a life 'free of sin' means.

2 You are going to collect information about how Puritans believed that people should live their lives – what they should and shouldn't do. As you read through this section, write your findings in a table like the one below.

Things people should do (how to live a godly life)	Things people shouldn't do (what makes a sinful life)

Making England 'free of sin'

Once they were in charge of running the country, the Puritans were determined to make England a place 'free of sin', so they began to make laws banning 'sinful' activities. Entertainment and enjoyment were 'out'; prayer, Bible-reading and good deeds were 'in'.

SOURCE A

A seventeenth-century illustration showing a Puritan family at mealtime.

SOURCE B

Puritan ideas about 'Works of Darkness' – sinful activities which should not be seen on a Sunday – and 'Works of Light', the way in which 'godly' people should spend their Sundays.

TASKS...

1. **a)** In what ways is the family meal shown in Source A different from a family meal today? Write down as many differences as you can, then compare lists with someone else.

   b) Which meal do you think you would prefer? Explain your reasons.

   c) From what you know about Protestant ideas, try to think of reasons why a Puritan family meal would be like this. Use your findings to add to your table about godly and sinful activities.

2. Look at Source B. Use the information in the picture to decide what the Puritans thought people should and should not do on a Sunday. Add this to your table.

TASKS...

3 Decide whether the activities below should be classed as 'Works of Darkness' (wrong to do on Sundays) or 'Works of Light' (things which should be done on Sundays) and add them to your table.

Horse-racing	Cock-fighting
Giving a sermon at dinner	Going to the theatre
Giving presents to the elderly	Gambling
Drinking alcohol in a pub	Dancing
Going for a walk	Walking to church
Doing the housework	Mending clothes
Celebrating Christmas	

Which of the activities you have learned about so far do you think might actually stop people from living good lives? Explain your choice to someone else in your class.

SOURCE C

Friday the Four and twentieth day of December, 1652.

Resolved by the Parliament,

That the Markets be kept to Morrow, being the Five and twentieth day of December; And that the Lord Major, and Sheriffs of London and Middlesex, and the Justices of Peace for the City of Westminster and Liberties thereof, do take care, That all such persons as shall open their Shops on that day, be protected from Wrong or Violence, and the Offenders punished.

Resolved by the Parliament,

That no Observation shall be had of the Five and twentieth day of December, commonly called Christmas-Day; nor any Solemnity used or exercised in Churches upon that Day in respect thereof.

Ordered by the Parliament,

That the Lord Major of the City of London, and Sheriffs of London and Middlesex, and the Justices of Peace of Middlesex respectively, be Authorized and Required to see this Order duly observed within the late Lines of Communication, and weekly Bills of Mortality.

Hen: Scobell, Cleric. Parliamenti.

London, Printed by John Field, Printer to the Parliament of England. 1652.

The 1652 law banning the celebration of Christmas.

Celebrating Christmas is forbidden

In 1652 Parliament decided that it was 'ungodly' to celebrate Christmas (see Source C). You can see from Source D on page 69 that some people felt that this was going too far.

The Vindication of
CHRISTMAS
OR,
His Twelve Yeares Observations upon the
Times, concerning the lamentable Game called Sweep-
stake ; acted by General *Plunder*, and Major General *Tax*;
With his Exhortation to the people ; a description of that
oppressing Ringworm called *Excise* ; and the manner how
our high and mighty Christmas-Ale that formerly would
knock down *Hercules*, & trip up the heels of a Giant, strook
into a deep Consumption with a blow from *Westminster*.

Keep out, you
come not here;

O Sir, I bring
good cheere.

Old Christmas
welcome ; Do
not fear.

Imprinted at London for G. Horton, 1653.

A drawing called the 'Vindication of Christmas', which was produced in 1653. 'Vindication' is when something is defended.

TASKS...

1 Working in groups, discuss the following questions using the information you have learnt about the Puritans:

a) Why do you think Parliament banned the celebration of Christmas?

b) When soldiers, acting on the government's orders, visited people's houses on Christmas Day and took Christmas dinner out of their ovens, do you think it would have changed people's attitudes towards Christmas? Why?

c) Do you think that banning the celebration of Christmas would have changed people's attitudes towards religion? Why?

d) Do you think that banning the celebration of Christmas would have changed people's attitudes towards Parliament?

Plenary

You have now collected enough information to give you a good picture of how the Puritans tried to make people live more godly lives. Note down three things you think would have been successful and three things you think would not have worked. Explain why you have selected each one.

WHY WERE THERE SO MANY DIFFERENT RELIGIOUS GROUPS AT THIS TIME? WHAT DID THEY BELIEVE?

Objectives

By the end of this section you will:

- know that many different religious groups sprang up after the Civil War
- understand some of the differences between the various groups
- be able to analyse and evaluate the evidence of sources.

SOURCE A

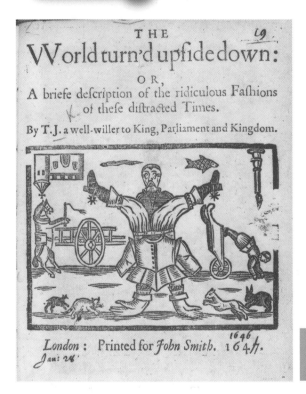

A cartoon titled 'The World turn'd upside down' published in 1647.

Starter

The cartoon in Source A is from a pamphlet published in 1647. It shows one person's reaction to the Civil War and the changes it brought to people.

What things can you think of that had been 'turn'd upside down' by the Civil War? Make a list. Why have you chosen each of the items on your list?

Why did so many different religious groups appear during and after the Civil War?

Since the first official translation of the Bible into English in 1539 (see page 21), printing presses had made it possible for many people to own a copy. It was not surprising that in the chaotic and frightening world of the 1650s many people turned to the Bible for guidance.

Protestants said that people did not need a priest to interpret the Bible for them – they could do this for themselves. Many people believed that the Bible was the source of all true knowledge. They thought that studying it could provide the answers to all of life's problems. However, the Bible is a long and complex book and different people found different answers in it.

💡 Make a list of all the places or people we can go to today to help us find the 'answers to life's problems'. Which of them do you think existed in the seventeenth century?

Everybody interpreting the Bible for themselves led to many strange beliefs and events. Several pregnant women claimed to be about to give birth to the Messiah – the Christian saviour. A lot of people believed that the 1650s would see the second coming of Christ. A man called James Nayler rode into Bristol on a donkey just like Jesus had done in the Holy Land. Women laid palm leaves in his path – just like when Jesus entered Jerusalem. Nayler was arrested and punished very severely, finally being thrown into prison, where he died.

What were the different religious groups?

After the Civil War lots of different religious groups, or sects, sprang up. Some, like the Baptists and The Society of Friends, still exist today. Others, like the Aposticals, the Fifth Monarchists and the Familists, did not last very long.

Cromwell's Puritan government was concerned about the beliefs of some of the new religious groups.

The Anabaptists, or Baptists as they became known, believed that people would be 'born again' if they were baptised as adults. This was following the example of Jesus, who had been 'born again' when he was baptised by John the Baptist as an adult. Baptists tried to set up their own closed communities and were sometimes known for defending their beliefs with violence.

Adamites believed in getting back to nature like the first human beings – Adam and Eve. Unlike other people at the time, they did not think that the human body should be kept hidden from view.

Familists thought that heaven and hell were real places and could be found in this world. They based their religion on love and the family.

Seekers were looking for the perfect Church and so tried lots of different ones but found none of them to their liking.

The Society of Friends was founded by George Fox in the early 1650s. Its followers believed that the spirit of brotherly love would inspire people and there was no need for organised churches with set services. At their meetings they waited for inspiration and often went into a trance, shaking with emotion. This led to their nickname – the Quakers.

The Ranters said that people who had been chosen by God could not sin, so it was all right to behave in any way they wished. They shocked people with their ideas about free love, drinking, smoking and swearing, all of which they carried out quite openly.

The Fifth Monarchists believed that there had been four kingdoms, or eras, in history and that the execution of Charles I in 1649 was the start of the Fifth Monarchy, which would see the Second Coming of the Messiah and the reign of Christ on earth. They thought that Cromwell's **republic** was a betrayal of this idea as it allowed Cromwell to run the country like a king.

Key words

Republic A country that is not ruled by a king or queen, but by a government elected by the citizens.

💡 Which of these religious groups do you think the government would have felt was acceptable? Why did you choose these?

💡 Which groups would it not have liked? Why do you think this?

SOURCE B

A print dated 1644 showing some of the religious sects which existed in the seventeenth century.

Licenfed according to order, and publifhed by M. *Stubs*, a late fellow-Ranter

Increase multiply

VVe have over com the Devil

No way to the old way

ey for Chrift mas

Imprinted at London, by J. C. MDCL. 1650

A seventeenth century illustration of the Ranters.

TASKS...

1 Draw a line like the one below and see if you can rank the different religious groups as the government might have viewed them.

Complete approval ●━━━━━━━━━━━━━━━━━━━━━━━━━━━● Complete disapproval

EXTENSION TASK

2 Find out two things about The Society of Friends today which make it different from other Protestant groups.

Case study: The Levellers

Some of the different religious groups' ideas about how to change things did not stop at religion. Some of them wanted to alter the way the country was governed. This made them very dangerous as far as the government was concerned. One of the groups thought to be the most dangerous, according to Oliver Cromwell, was the Levellers.

TASKS...

1 In order to find out how dangerous the Levellers were, what questions do you think Oliver Cromwell would have asked about them? Draw up a list.

2 Now see if you can find the answers to your questions from the evidence shown in the boxes below.
Write down your answers.

The evidence

Many Levellers lived in London. Among them were shopkeepers and apprentices. There were many Levellers in Cromwell's New Model Army which had recently defeated Charles I. Many soldiers had not been paid by Parliament for months. They felt resentful that they had helped to defeat the king but were not being rewarded for their efforts.

The Levellers were led by John Lilburne. He had served Parliament in the army for a short time before quarrelling with his commanding officer. He was put on trial for treason in 1649 when he criticised Cromwell and Parliament. He was found not guilty. However, he continued to criticise the government. He was **banished** in 1651 but after returning to England in 1653 was put in prison where he died in 1657.

After the king's execution there was a lot of unrest. A Leveller soldier was shot for mutiny. His funeral in London turned into a demonstration. The mourners wore green ribbons – the Leveller colour.

Colonel Rainsborough, an important Leveller, said: 'I think that the poorest man that is in England has a life to live as the greatest man; every man that is to live under a government ought first to agree to put himself under that government.'

The Levellers put some demands to Parliament in May 1649. These included the following:
* Parliament should be chosen by men over 21.
* People accused of crimes should be tried by jury.
* People should be allowed freedom of worship.
* The death penalty should be for murder only.
* The people of each **parish** should choose their own ministers.
* No person accused of a crime should be forced to give evidence against themselves.
* All money for the government should be raised by taxing property.

The harvest of 1649 was very poor. In the winter, poor people suffered greatly from high prices and a shortage of grain. Many people had thought that with the defeat and execution of the king there would be a better life for ordinary people. Now it seemed as if life was just as bad, if not worse.

Key words

Banish To stop somebody from living in their country.
Parish The area around a church.

TASKS...

1 Copy out and fill in the speech bubbles below to show what different people thought of the Levellers. You will need to show that you understand what each person would have said if they had been asked about their views. Consider all the evidence before you begin. **WS**

I just manage to scrape a living and so I think ...

I'm used to having a say in how the country should be run and so I think ...

A woman who lives in a small village and who farms the land for her living.

A rich landowner.

Now that the king has gone, I have even more power and so I think ...

I helped to put this country where it is today and so I think ...

An MP who is a Puritan.

A soldier of the New Model Army who hasn't been paid for months.

Cromwell had to decide what, if anything, should be done about the Levellers.

💡 Do any of your important questions remain unanswered? What would you have decided?

What happened to the Levellers?

In 1649, 1200 Levellers attempted to overthrow the government but were cornered by 2000 troops led by Cromwell in Burford, Oxfordshire. Most of the rebels fled or surrendered, but 340 rebels were imprisoned in Burford church for three days. Then, three Leveller soldiers were shot dead in front of the others. The Leveller revolt was over.

Plenary

Here are the answers! Work out the questions.

1　Baptists and The Society of Friends.

2　The Fifth Monarchists.

3　Because they hadn't been paid.

4　Trial by jury, freedom of worship and no accused person to be forced to give evidence against themselves.

WHAT DIFFERENT PROBLEMS DID JAMES I AND JAMES II FACE IN THE SEVENTEENTH CENTURY?

WAS GUY FAWKES FRAMED?

Objectives

In this section you will:
- look at different views and interpretations of the Gunpowder Plot
- try to decide whether you think Guy Fawkes was framed.

Starter

SOURCE A

A print from the time showing the execution of the Gunpowder plotters. After their trial for treason they were hanged, drawn and quartered.

Imagine that there was television in 1605. You are a reporter at the execution of the plotters shown in Source A. Prepare a one-minute presentation describing the scene to viewers of a national news programme.

The Gunpowder Plot

On 5 November 1605 James I was due to open his first Parliament. The Lords and MPs were to gather in the House of Lords to hear him speak. King James and his government were Protestant. However, on the evening of 4 November a message was passed to Lord Monteagle, a Catholic, advising him not to go to Parliament. Lord Monteagle showed the letter to Robert Cecil, who was James's chief adviser. Cecil sent guards to search the Parliament building and in the cellar under the House of Lords they found 36 barrels of gunpowder. They also found a man who was preparing to light the fuse when Parliament met – his name was Guy Fawkes and he was a Catholic.

Historians agree that gunpowder was found in the cellar on 4 November. They also agree that Guy Fawkes was preparing for the explosion the next day when he was arrested. However, there are two different theories about the Gunpowder Plot.

Theory 1

Robert Cecil found out just in time about the plot only because of the message to Lord Monteagle.

Theory 2

Robert Cecil knew about the plot beforehand through spies and allowed the plotters to go ahead. He even made it easy for them to get gunpowder from a government store so that he could catch them in the act. He did this so that he would have an excuse to **persecute** Catholics in England.

Key words

Persecute To cause people to suffer because of their beliefs.

TASKS...

1 In groups, look at the evidence shown in Sources B–H on pages 79–80. Which evidence supports:
   - Theory 1?
   - Theory 2?
   Write your answers in your book.

SOURCE B

My Lord, I have a care for your safety. Therefore I would advise you to devise some excuse to miss your attendance at this Parliament. For God and man have come together to punish the wickedness of this time. Go into the country, for they shall receive a terrible blow this Parliament – and yet they shall not see who hurts them.

An extract from the letter delivered to the house of Lord Monteagle by a disguised messenger on 26 October 1605.

SOURCE C

He said he did not intend to set fire to the fuse until the King came into the Houses of Parliament, and then he intended to do it so that the powder might blow up a quarter of an hour later.

From the confession of Guy Fawkes after he had been tortured on the rack.

SOURCE D

Two signatures by Guy Fawkes. The first is his usual signature. The second is from his confession after being tortured.

SOURCE E

The plan was the idea of Robert Catesby, a Catholic. Along with other Catholic gentlemen, they would blow up the Houses of Parliament when King James I went there to make a speech. At 7 o'clock on 26 October, Lord Monteagle was about to have dinner when one of his servants brought him a letter. It had been given to him by a stranger in the street. The letter was written by Francis Tresham, one of the plotters and Lord Monteagle's cousin. The letter warned him not to attend Parliament. Monteagle did not know what to make of it. Even so, he took it at once to Robert Cecil, the King's chief minister. Cecil took the letter to the King.

On 4 November, the cellar was searched. They found gunpowder and John Johnson was arrested. In the Tower of London he was tortured and admitted that he was Guy Fawkes. He confessed about the plot on 8 November.

Robert Cecil's description of the events of the Gunpowder Plot .

SOURCE F

A seventeenth-century drawing showing how Britain was saved from 'Catholic plots'. On the left can be seen the Spanish Armada; in the centre, the Pope and his cardinals plotting; and on the right, Guy Fawkes in the cellar – but with God watching him.

SOURCE G

Here are more details about the Gunpowder Plot:

- Cecil's spies were constantly watching Catholics.
- The cellar where the gunpowder was stored was owned by a government official.
- At the time the government controlled all gunpowder. All supplies were kept in the Tower of London. How did the plotters get their supplies? Cecil forbade any investigation into the Tower stores beyond early 1604.
- Was the letter to Monteagle a forgery?
- Monteagle's name was removed from all accounts about the plot. He was given a pension by the government.
- When the plotters were arrested on 7 November, the government seemed to have known in advance where all the plotters were.
- All the plotters were killed or executed except Francis Tresham. He died in December 1605 in the Tower of London from an unknown illness.

An extract from a modern textbook.

SOURCE H

Some hold it as certain that there was foul play and that some of the government secretly spun a web to entangle these poor gentlemen.

Written by an Italian Catholic visitor in 1605.

TASKS...

1 a) In groups, do a reliability check on each of the Sources B–H to decide how far you can trust them. Use the 5Ws:

- *Who* wrote or drew it? Would they be biased?
- *Why* did they write or draw it?
- *What* were they trying to make people think or believe?
- *When* was it written or drawn?
- *Where* did they get their information from?

b) Make a copy of the table below and give each source a rating of 1–5 (1 = totally unreliable; 5 = very reliable). Briefly explain your decision in each case.

Source	Rating (1–5)	Reason

2 Now that you have considered the reliability of each source, think about the key question again:

Was Guy Fawkes framed?

You could use the following guide to help with your answer.

- Write an introduction that sets out the issue and states your aims.
- Put each new point in a separate paragraph. Start each paragraph with a sentence that introduces the point you are going to make clearly and directly.
- Support the argument in each paragraph by adding detailed evidence from your reading.
- Use quotes from your reading to support your arguments.
- Write in the third person and the past tense when you are describing events and changes, and in the first person and the present tense when you are giving your personal views.
- Use connectives. For example when comparing and contrasting, use words like *equally, similarly, likewise, whereas, instead of*.
- When supporting your views with evidence, use words like *such as, for instance, as revealed by*.
- Write a summary and conclusion that sets out your overall opinion about the question.
- Look at the marking scheme which your teacher will show you, to gain clues about how to be successful in your essay.

Plenary

Here are the answers! Work out the questions.

1 To blow up the king and the House of Lords.

2 James I introduced fines on Catholics.

3 The letter warned Lord Monteagle not to go to the House of Lords.

4 Catholics became even more unpopular.

WAS THE 'GLORIOUS REVOLUTION' INEVITABLE?

Objectives

In this section you will try to decide:
- why James II upset so many people
- whether he could have prevented the 'Glorious Revolution'.

Starter

Read Source A.

SOURCE **A**

> Imagine a group of Catholics attacking your wives and daughters, smashing your little children's brains against the walls or cutting your throats. Imagine seeing your mother or father tied to the stake in the midst of flames. This is what people saw the last time Catholics ruled us.

An extract from a pamphlet printed in London in 1679.

What image do you get of Catholics from this pamphlet? According to Source A, would a Catholic king be popular in England?

Key words

Revolution The forcible overthrow of a government.

The 'Glorious Revolution'

As you read the following text, try to work out why the 'Glorious **Revolution**' took place.

The events of 1688 have been called the 'Glorious Revolution'. The English removed an unpopular monarch, James II. This was done peacefully, without a civil war (as there had been during the reign of Charles I – see pages 43 to 64). Parliament simply asked James II's daughter and son-in-law, William and Mary of Orange, to come to England and rule as King and Queen instead of James II. William and Mary agreed, and in November 1688 William landed at Brixham in Devon and marched towards London.

Why did the English Parliment want to replace James II? The Glorious Revolution took place because, during his brief reign, James II succeeded in upsetting a great number of his subjects.

How did James II upset so many people?

Marriage
In 1672 James II declared himself a Catholic and married for a second time. His new wife, Mary of Modena, was also a Catholic.

Archbishop and bishops
From April 1687 James allowed all Christians, including Catholics, to worship as they wished. The Archbishop of Canterbury and six other bishops protested against these changes. James II had them arrested and put on trial. In August 1688 the court found them not guilty. There were celebrations, including bonfires, all over London as this was the first time that an English king had lost a court case.

Catholics
From 1687 James II allowed Catholics to worship openly. He appointed Catholics as ministers and officers in the army – all without the permission of Parliament.

The 'warming pan' baby
In June 1688 Mary of Modena gave birth to a son. This meant that James II now had a male heir who would be Catholic. However, there were doubts as to whether the baby really was the king and queen's child. James II was over 50 years old and his wife had already had several miscarriages. Rumours spread that the baby had actually been smuggled into the palace in a **warming pan**.

Monmouth Rebellion
In 1685 James II cruelly crushed a Protestant rebellion led by the Duke of Monmouth, who was Charles II's illigitimate son. About 250 men and women were hanged, drawn and quartered. A further 1000 people were sent away to the West Indies where they were sold as slaves.

Standing army
James II used the excuse of the Monmouth Rebellion to build up a large army which he stationed just outside London.

Government
James began appointing Catholics as government ministers and sacked all ministers who opposed him.

SOURCE B

The Queen is brought to bed of a Boy

Reported So

A playing card of 1689, showing how the baby might have been secretly smuggled into the palace.

Key words
Warming pan A pan to warm the bed, usually filled with coals.

TASKS...

1 Create a mind map to show why the 'Glorious Revolution' took place. Be ready to explain your links.

2 Imagine that you are an adviser to James II in 1685–8. What advice would you give him to prevent the 'Glorious Revolution'? Write out your advice in the form of a memo to the king.

Memo

To: King James II
From:
Date:
Subject:

To avoid a possible revolution I suggest that...

Plenary

Write a headline for a tabloid newspaper article which announces that James II is no longer king. Try to use alliteration in your headline.

HOW 'GLORIOUS' WAS THE REVOLUTION?

Objectives

In this section you will try to decide answers to the following questions:
- How peaceful was the revolution?
- How much change did it bring?

Starter

SOURCE A

A painting showing William and his troops landing in Brixham, Devon, in 1688.

SOURCE B

A Dutch engraving of the Revolution of 1688 with William and Mary on the right.

What impression do Sources A and B give of the 'Glorious Revolution'? How are they different? Why do you think they are so different?

The 'Glorious Revolution' – the events

The revolution of 1688 was seen as 'Glorious' because it was peaceful and popular with almost everyone and it reduced the power of the monarchy.

TASKS...

1 Look at the statements about the Glorious Revolution below. Organise them into two lists, supporting or opposing the description of the revolution as 'Glorious'. Beware! Some of the statements may be 'red herrings'. Leave these out. **WS**

1 Powerful people invited William of Orange, Prince of the Netherlands, to invade England and make himself king.

2 William and Mary were Protestants and were far more popular than the Catholic James II.

3 On 20 December 1688 James II secretly sent his wife and baby to France.

4 Under William and Mary, Parliament was given the power to raise taxes, pass laws and control the army.

5 On 4 November 1688 William landed at Brixham in Devon with 15,000 Dutch and English soldiers. William and his men marched steadily towards London, cheered on their way as 'Protestant saviours'. They were joined by supporters who pinned orange colours on their shirts.

6 In 1689 James II landed in Ireland and began to help the Irish Catholics. He took land back from the Protestant settlers who were alarmed and angry at this.

7 In 1689 William and Mary were presented with the Bill of Rights. This said that they had to obey the laws of England and could only change them with Parliament's permission.

8 James II died in 1702.

9 In December 1688 William marched to within 25 kilometres of Windsor. He wanted James II to be seen to leave freely. He did not want to force him out.

10 In 1689 in Ireland many Protestants fled to Londonderry to get away from James II and his troops. They surrounded the city and blocked off the port. The *siege* lasted for 105 days. About 15,000 Protestants died during the siege of Londonderry, including nearly all the children.

11 William and Mary had not become monarchs through **birthright**. Parliament had invited them to become rulers of England.

12 The Bill of Rights said that Parliament had to meet at least every three years.

13 Eventually, in December 1688, William sent his troops to London. They took over Whitehall Palace. For one night James II was guarded by William's troops. The next day James left for France.

14 William came to England because he wanted to become more powerful. He hoped to get the support of England for the Dutch in their war against the Catholic King of France, Louis XIV.

15 James II's first wife died in 1671. They had two daughters, Mary and Anne.

16 William went to Ireland with an army in 1690 and defeated James II's Catholic army at the Battle of the Boyne on 1 July 1690.

17 As king, William needed money from the English Parliament to help pay for his war with France. In return, he had to allow greater powers for Parliament.

18 After the defeat of James II in Ireland, William was popular with Irish Protestants but not with Irish Catholics. Over 4000 Catholics lost their land and Catholics were not allowed to be soldiers, teachers or town councillors.

19 The Bill of Rights said that no Catholic could ever become King of England.

20 In 1694 **Noncomformists** were allowed to worship freely.

Key words

Siege A military blockade of a city.
Birthright A right or title to which someone is entitled by birth.
Nonconformist Any Protestant who was not a member of the Church of England.

TASKS...

1 Now make a judgement – how 'Glorious' was the revolution? You will need to write at least three paragraphs, one for each of the reasons for the description 'Glorious'. For example:
   - peaceful
   - popular
   - a return to monarchy.

2 Do you think 'Glorious' is the right word to describe the revolution? If not, suggest a better word to describe the revolution.

Plenary

Draw a sketch to represent the changes in the position of the monarchy as a result of the 'Glorious Revolution'. Compare it with someone else's in your class. Are there any similarities and/or differences? Why?

THEME: RELIGION AND INTERNAL POLITICS

CONCLUSION

Before you started this theme you might have thought it was odd to put religion and politics together. Now that you have finished it you can see that they were so closely bound together that it is often almost impossible to see where one ends and the other begins. Was Elizabeth I's quarrel with Philip II of Spain about religion or about politics? Were the causes of the Civil War religious - or political?

The official religion of England changed according to the beliefs of the king or queen. When the ruler of the country was Catholic, then everyone had to be Catholic, as in Mary I's reign. When the ruler was Protestant, then the official religion of the country was Protestant, for example in James I's reign.

You can get an overview of how religion and politics affected each other in the period 1500-1570 by creating your own timeline.

Using a piece of landscape A3 paper plot on it:

- the reigns of each ruler
- examples of when politics and religion overlap.

An example has been started for you below.

Ruler	James II, 1685-8
Main Religion	Catholic
Political Events	Monmouth Rebellion, 1685 Glorious Revolution, 1688

Leave space at the bottom to add some more rows for each ruler. You can then add in information from the next two themes which will help you to build up your timeline into a comprehensive overview of the whole period.

THEME: SOCIAL LIFE

INTRODUCTION

Are you upper class, middle class or working class? Does it matter to you? Your answer will probably relate to how wealthy you are. It tends to be money that is important to people these days rather than position in society, but in the sixteenth and seventeenth centuries it was both position and money that mattered. Your social class determined where you lived, how you dressed, what job you did, what you ate, how much money you had – in fact everything about you. It could make a difference between having a good life and a poor one.

Five hundred years ago people's lives were very different from ours. Ordinary people had to work very hard in order simply to survive. Their daily routines were all about getting enough food on the table.

Rich people had better homes and food but they still faced the same diseases. They might live better from day to day but many of them still died young. Women were particularly at risk during childbirth.

Life was difficult and dangerous and sometimes lawless. There was no police force and crime was punished harshly. Plotting against the monarch, stealing, begging and witchcraft might all be punished by execution. After all, death was an everyday occurrence. People were used to pain so it was not surprising that it was inflicted as a punishment.

All this doesn't mean that people lived dull and depressing lives. Most people were able to have fun and enjoyed their leisure time, even though they didn't have televisions or computers. Pleasures were simple. People's lives were well ordered and everybody knew where they stood in society.

6 HOW DID PEOPLE LIVE IN THE SIXTEENTH AND SEVENTEENTH CENTURIES?

HOW WERE PEOPLE DIVIDED IN SOCIETY?

By the end of this section you will understand:
- how people were divided by class
- that each of the four main classes lived very different lives.

You will be able to :
- describe the lifestyle of each of the four main classes.

Starter

Think about the things in your home that you couldn't live without.

💡 *Brainstorm a list of items in your home which are essential for basic living.*

💡 *Brainstorm a list of things which you think of as luxuries – the things you could live without if you had to.*

💡 *Compare your lists with others in your class.*

People living in Tudor times also had essentials and luxuries. Some of these are shown below.
- *Which do you think are essentials?*
- *Which do you think are luxuries?*

Sort them into two groups.

Window glass	Wax candles	Mattresses
	Cooking pots	
Silk and velvet clothes		Linen clothes
	Room for all the family	
Room for the animals in winter		Fire for cooking
	Feather bed	
Toys		Woollen clothes
	Separate rooms for sleeping and living	

Which different classes of people existed in Tudor and Stuart times?

A churchman called William Harrison, who lived in Elizabeth I's reign, described English people like this:

> *We in England divide our people into four sorts: gentlemen,[1] citizens or burgesses,[2] yeomen[3] and labourers.[4]*

By this, he meant:

1 *noblemen* – lords and other rich people who owned land and had many servants.

2 *well-off town-dwellers* – usually merchants and traders.

3 *farmers* – who owned or rented their own land and perhaps employed some people to work for them.

4 *poor labourers* – farm workers who worked for landowners and perhaps also rented a little land on which they could grow their own food.

TASKS...

1 Look at the pictures of the gentleman, citizen, yeoman and labourer. Write down which of the descriptions goes with each picture.

How could each class be recognised?

| **A gentleman.** | **A citizen.** | **A yeoman.** | **A labourer.** |

A He lives in a small village and rarely travels outside it, as the only form of transport for him is walking. Once or twice a year he might visit a travelling fair to buy the things that can't be made in the village. He works very hard – ploughing, weeding, looking after animals, mending fences and in fact doing anything he's told to do on the lord's farm.

B He has a country estate consisting of a large mansion with beautiful grounds and farms that provide for all his family's needs. He spends a lot of time in London at the king or queen's court, leaving his wife and family in the country. It can be quite a lonely life for them.

C He lives quite a comfortable existence, although he isn't important enough to mix socially with the nobility. He owns some land and rents more. He works very hard but can afford to send his children to school.

D He lives in the town and makes quite a lot of money trading in cloth and also from supplying all the things that the growing population needs. He has a big house which also serves as his office. He stores quite a lot of goods there, too. He plays an important role in organising how the town is run.

The class system in England at this time was very rigid – it was difficult to move up into a higher class, even if you had made a lot of money. People from each class could be recognised by their homes, their jobs and even by the clothes they wore. There were laws which made it illegal for the three lower classes – citizen, yeoman and labourer – to wear the clothes of a higher class, even if they could afford to.

SOURCE A

A painting of guests at a wedding celebration just outside London in the sixteenth century.

Which of the 'four sorts' or classes can you see in Source A?
What are they doing?

TASKS...

1 Look at Sources B–K. Then decide which sources match each social class. What do they tell us about the people of each social class? Use the information you have read to help you.

2 Copy the table below, and write in your answers. **WS**

Class	Sources describing each class	What the sources tell us
Gentlemen		
Citizens		
Yeomen		
Labourers		

SOURCE B

My father was a yeoman. He had no lands of his own but rented a farm for £3 or £4 a year. He farmed as much as half a dozen men. He had grazing for 100 sheep and my mother milked 30 cows. He sent me to school. He was generous to poor neighbours and he gave to the poor.

Bishop Hugh Latimer speaking in the early sixteenth century.

SOURCE C

This house was built in Suffolk in the late sixteenth century.

SOURCE D

The interior of a house built at the end of the sixteenth century.

SOURCE E

The Earl of Arundel entered, all in gilt and engraved armour, with four **pages** and 22 gentlemen, all dressed in cloaks and **breeches** of red velvet, laid with gold lace, jackets of yellow satin, caps of red velvet with yellow feathers and yellow silk stockings.

Description of clothes worn to a tournament in 1651.

Key words

Page A young man who is a personal servant to a wealthy person.
Breeches Short trousers that go down to just below the knee.
Tournament A sporting event for knights.

SOURCE F

A contemporary drawing of a home built in the eighteenth century.

SOURCE G

Citizens and burgesses are those that are free within cities and are rich enough to hold office there.

William Harrison writing in the late sixteen century.

SOURCE H

Working in the fields, shown in a seventeenth century painting.

The bedroom of a house built during the seventeenth century.

The fourth and last sort of people in England are day labourers, poor farmworkers and all wage earners such as tailors, shoemakers and carpenters.

William Harrison.

A home built during the late sixteenth century.

TASKS...

Work in a group.

1. Choose one social class. Draw up a list to show:
   a) all the good things about being this 'sort'
   b) all the bad things.

2. Now, create a profile for a member of this social group.

You should include their:
- name, date of birth and address
- education and training
- jobs held/experience
- manners and behaviour.

If you have time, you could illustrate your work.

Plenary

Write a list of six things that you would like to know about the four classes of people in England. Where would you go to find out these things?

Compare your list with the rest of the class and work in groups to research the most frequently asked questions.

HOW DID PEOPLE ENJOY THEIR LEISURE TIME?

Objectives

By the end of this section you will know:
- which different sports and entertainments were available to rich and poor people
- how far the sort of sports and entertainments people enjoyed depended on their social class.

You will be able to:
- use sources to work out the differences between the leisure activities of the rich and the poor.

Starter

💡 *Identify as many games as you can in Source A.*

💡 *Which of these games are still played today?*

SOURCE A

A painting showing a variety of games which were popular in the sixteenth century.

Which types of sport and entertainment existed, and who enjoyed them?

TASKS...

1. As you study the information in this section, try to identify the different types of sport and entertainment. Divide them into:
   a) activities that people take part in
   b) activities where people are spectators.

2. Try to decide which activities would have been enjoyed by:
   a) rich people   b) poor people.
   Are there any which would have been for both?

Everyone seeks to overthrow his opponent and throw him on the nose, even on hard stone. He doesn't care as long as he gets him down. Sometimes their necks are broken, sometimes their legs, sometimes their arms, sometimes their noses gush out with blood. Everyone is wounded and bruised.

Football was played in both town and country. The object was to get the ball into your own parish. It was very violent, as this spectator noted.

In the countryside, hunting was an activity enjoyed by almost all classes. While the richer people rode, the less well-off went on foot after the hunt – or went **poaching** for rabbits and hares on their lord's land. Laws were passed to try to stop this illegal form of hunting. At Christmas time, a huge Yule log burned in the great hall of the manor and for the twelve days of Christmas the lord entertained his rich friends and the poor of the village. There was feasting, dancing, games of all sorts and singing by individuals and groups.

An extract from a modern history book on Tudor England.

Key words

Poaching Killing and stealing animals (for example, pheasants, deer or rabbits) from a rich person's land.

Queen Elizabeth I's reign was a time when the theatre became very popular. Plays had been performed for centuries, but mostly out in the open on portable stages or in the great halls in manor houses. Now many theatres were built, like the Globe and the Rose in London, and going to see a play became a popular social event for all classes. William Shakespeare, Christopher Marlowe, Ben Jonson, Thomas Kyd and many other famous playwrights had their plays performed in Elizabeth I's time.

A drawing of the old Swan Theatre in the late sixteenth century.

21 December 1663
Went to Shoe Lane to see a cock-fight at a new pit there. Saw a strange variety of people from Members of Parliament to the poorest apprentices, bakers, brewers, butchers, delivery men and so on. And all of them swearing and betting.

An extract from The Diary of Samuel Pepys.

The last opportunity for fun before the fasting of Lent was known as Shrovetide (we still celebrate Shrove Tuesday with pancakes). It was a dull and difficult time of the year and food supplies would be running low. It was then that 'threshing the cock' took place (Source F).

All classes of people enjoyed dancing. It was important to be able to dance as it was the main way in which men and women met each other.

SOURCE F

A cockerel was tethered with a string and then people tried to kill it by throwing things at it. If you killed the cock you won it as a prize. Sometimes the cock would be buried with just its head sticking out of the ground and then blindfolded people would try to kill it with a **flail**.

A contemporary description of 'threshing the cock'.

SOURCE G

Dancing is practised to reveal whether lovers are in good health and sound of limb. After dancing they are permitted to kiss each other in order that they can tell if they are shapely or give off an unpleasant smell, like bad meat.

From an instruction book on dancing by a Frenchman, Thoinoit Arbeau.

SOURCE H

A painting showing Elizabeth I dancing at court with Robert Dudley, Earl of Leicester.

Fairs were rare events and offered the opportunity for a lot of fun for all classes. There would be jugglers, acrobats, fire-eaters, musicians and all sorts of performing players. There was plenty of food and drink as well as games and gambling. There was also the opportunity to wonder at foreign and exotic people and goods.

Key words

Bait To harass a chained animal with dogs.

A large bear on a long rope was bound to a stake, then a number of great English fighting dogs were brought in and shown first to the bear, which they afterwards used to **bait** one after another. The bear's teeth were not so sharp they could injure the dogs; they had broken them short. When the first bear was tired another was supplied and fresh dogs to bait him. Only when the dogs had overpowered the bear did people come to its aid.

Thomas Platter, a German visitor to London, writing in 1599. Elizabeth I used to enjoy entertainments such as bear-baiting.

A contemporary illustration of a fair in the seventeenth century.

TASKS...

1 Imagine that you are either a poor young man or a rich young lord in the time of Elizabeth I. You are able to swap identities for a week and enjoy the other's social life. Send a postcard home describing the entertainment you enjoy.

Plenary

Explain in two paragraphs what you would have enjoyed or disliked about Tudor and Stuart entertainment, and why.

HOW HARD WAS LIFE FOR WOMEN?

Objectives

By the end of this section, you will know:
- why a lot of women lived hard and difficult lives
- why women had few rights and faced many difficulties and dangers in their lives, whatever their position in society
- why some women were independent and successful.

You will be able to:
- make value judgements based on historical evidence
- explain the roles of some sixteenth- and seventeenth-century women.

Starter

From what you know about life in the sixteenth and seventeenth centuries, where do you think you would stand on this line?

Women lived poor and
miserable lives.

Women lived satisfying and
happy lives.

 Make a note of where you think you would stand and give a reason for your decision.

When you have completed your study of the role of women at this time, you will again be asked where you think you would stand. You will need to give more reasons for your decision – reasons based on historical evidence.

What was the place of women in society?

The information and Sources A–R examine:
- different people's attitudes towards women
- women's rights
- how women spent their time
- the problems women faced.

They will give you a fuller picture of the difficulties and dangers women faced in their lives in the sixteenth and seventeenth centuries.

TASKS...

1. Using the information and sources on each of the topics about women, write down one or two statements to sum up the main ideas.

2. Then note down an example to explain or describe each idea. You could organise your ideas in a table, or in a spider diagram like the one below. ◆ **WS**

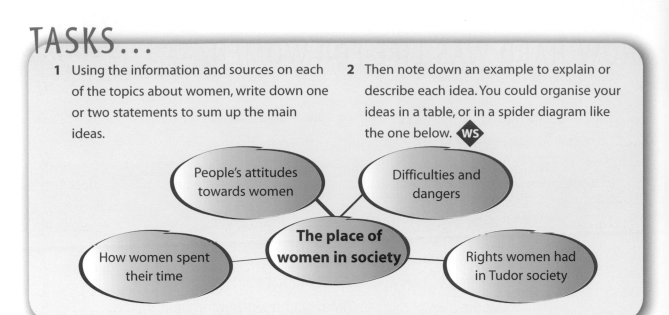

- People's attitudes towards women
- Difficulties and dangers
- **The place of women in society**
- How women spent their time
- Rights women had in Tudor society

What were people's attitudes toward women?

In a Tudor home the wife was in charge of running the household. However, if something displeased her husband, she would be held to blame. A man could legally beat his wife, although the stick he used was not supposed to be thicker than his thumb.

A modern historian.

A cartoon from the late sixteenth century showing a husband beating his wife.

To educate women and tame foxes has the same effect: it makes them more cunning.

King James I is reported to have said this about women.

The husband is the highest person in the family and has authority over everyone else. He is a king in his own house.

An extract from a book, *Of Domestical Duties*, written in 1622 by William Gouge.

SOURCE E

28 February 1665

I checked my wife's kitchen accounts at the end of the month and found 7 shillings missing. This caused us to fall out. I called her 'beggar' and she told me off … I find she is very cunning, and even though she does not show it, she is always plotting in her mind … We parted, after many cross words, very angry; and I went to my office.

An extract from The Diary of Samuel Pepys.

Key words

Poultice A bandage containing ointment to help injuries heal.
Revel To party.

SOURCE F

19 December 1664

I was very angry and began to find fault with my wife for not commanding her servants as she ought. Then, after she gave me a cross answer, I struck her over her left eye with such a blow that the poor wretch cried out and was in great pain. Yet her spirit was so strong that she tried to bite and scratch me … I was distressed to my heart to think what I had done, for she was forced to lay a **poultice** on her eye all day, and it is black – and the servants saw it.

An extract from The Diary of Samuel Pepys.

However, women were not only being kept in their place by men. Women, too, had a clear idea of how members of their own sex should behave.

SOURCE G

Too many women now behave like men … the war has led them to walk about with a superior attitude, to gamble, to drink, to **revel** and to quarrel.

The Duchess of Newcastle complaining about the behaviour of women after the Civil War.

What rights did women have in Tudor and Stuart society?

The position of women in Tudor times was very different from today. In 1500 women were second-class citizens and had almost no legal rights. When a woman got married her property became her husband's – including any children she might have.

Marriage

A woman rarely got to choose whether she married or stayed single. Her parents decided for her and often marriages were arranged, although this was less likely if she came from a poor family – then a woman might actually marry for love. Sometimes girls not yet in their teens would be married in name only and then whisked away from their new husbands. Husband and wife would be reunited when they were young adults – married, but strangers.

A woman had to bring a **dowry** with her when she married and this might be anything from a few sheep to vast lands and huge amounts of money. Marriages for women from richer households were really contracts agreed for reasons of wealth and status. Noble families also often agreed **alliances** with each other through marriage.

SOURCE H

A wealthy lady playing the spinet, by Giovanni Martinelli (1610–59).

How did women spend their time?

How women spent their days depended on their position in society.

The rich

A rich lady would not have to do housework or look after her children. She had servants to do those things for her. Instead, she would make sure that her most important servants were running the household properly. Her other daily tasks included checking on menus, reading, embroidery and making sure that everything was in order for when her husband came home from court or his business.

They spend time walking, riding, playing cards and visiting friends, talking to neighbours and making merry with them … England is called the paradise of married women.

A Dutch man's description of women's life in England in 1575.

A merchant's wife would probably have helped her husband to run his business as well as looking after the household. She would have worked hard but the rewards would have been great: a comfortable home, servants, fine clothes, good food and considerable respect in society.

The poor

In the countryside a poor woman would have helped her husband in the fields, cooked, looked after the children, spun wool or made lace (or whatever the local industry was) and mended clothes. In fact she would have turned her hand to whatever was necessary. It was a hard life and could be harder or easier depending on how wealthy her husband was. If he owned or rented a reasonable amount of land, then there would be servants to help her with her chores. If he was a labourer working for the local landowner then she would have to do everything herself. She would also have helped her husband with his work in the fields at busy times, such as harvest.

Key words

Winnow To shake out corn to separate the grain from the rest of the plant.
Shear To cut.

It is a wife's occupation to **winnow** corn, to make hay and **shear** corn. In time of need she should help her husband fill the muck waggon, drive the plough, load hay, go to market to sell butter, cheese, milk, eggs, chickens, pigs, geese and corn.

An extract from Anthony Fitzherbert's *Book of Husbandry*, written in 1523.

What difficulties and dangers did women face in their everyday lives?

People knew little about diseases and their cures and did not pay much attention to cleanliness and hygiene. Everybody was at risk from illness and disease. Marriages tended to be only a few years long because one of the partners would die.

The **infant mortality rate** was also very high – around one in three babies died before their first birthday. Childbirth was also extremely hazardous for women.

SOURCE K

The birth of a baby in the late sixteenth century. In the background, astrologers are recording the position of the planets at the time of birth.

Childbirth

People did not know how to deal with the complications which often arose in childbirth. They paid no attention to cleanliness because they did not know it was important. Childbed fever was extremely common. Money and fine living were no guarantee of survival, either. Two of Henry VIII's wives died in childbirth: Jane Seymour died days after the birth of the future Edward VI; Catherine Parr married again after Henry's death and died while giving birth.

SOURCE L

Mistress Earnshaw of York was in painful labour, and had her child pulled from her slowly. She died at last, leaving a sad husband.

This death in childbirth was recorded in 1684.

Pregnancy

Having a baby when you were not married was regarded as both sinful and shameful. A pregnant girl was often thrown out by her family. This meant she was doomed to a life of poverty – and often prostitution. Some girls tried to hide their pregnancy and then abandoned or killed their baby. If they were caught they could be hanged. The baby's father suffered no shame and did not have to support his child or the mother. Since there was no such thing as DNA testing he could always claim that the child was not his.

SOURCE M

I thank you for your good will, but I pray that you be content and speak no more to me of your love. My marriage depends wholly on my parents. For, if I am not ruled by them in my marriage they will no longer support me.

An extract from a letter written by a young lady to Thomas Wythorne, a court musician, in 1558. She did not marry him but later married a richer man of her parents' choice.

SOURCE N

When Edward VI lay dying without an heir the Duke of Northumberland decided that the 16-year-old Protestant, Lady Jane Grey, should succeed to the throne, rather than Edward's Catholic sister, Mary Tudor. In order to ensure he had control over her, Northumberland married Jane to his son, Guilford Dudley. However, Jane refused at first and was beaten by her father until she agreed.

A modern historian.

What control did women have over their own lives?

💡 Why did women get married? Surely it would have been better to remain single and independent?

Life for an unmarried woman could be very insecure. Without the protection of a husband, brother or father she would find it difficult to look after and support herself. Even if she had property, unless she had a very strong character, men would probably not take her seriously as a landowner. She might be cheated by her servants, her lands and property might be stolen, or she might be forced to marry. Most women did as their parents wanted and married the man they chose for them.

However, some women were determined to marry for love and stood up to their parents. As you can see from Source N, this was often a matter of physical as well as moral courage.

A woman who could not support herself was dependent on her nearest male relative to give her a roof over her head. She would probably be constantly reminded of the family's charity towards her. After the monasteries and convents had been closed down in Henry VIII's time, unsupported women could not even seek security in a religious house.

Some women tried to make ends meet by spinning wool. Many 'spinster' aunts lived with their relatives trying to contribute to the family's income in this way.

The women of England are fair and pretty. They have far more freedom than in other countries and know just how to make good use of it. They often stroll around or drive out by coach in beautiful clothes and then men have to put up with such behaviour and may not punish them for it. Indeed the good wives often beat their men.

An extract from Thomas Platter's *Travels in England*, written in 1599.

SOURCE P

A portrait of Bess of Hardwick (1520–1608).

Could women ever be independent and successful?

Bess of Hardwick was brought up in the sixteenth century. As a gentleman's daughter she would probably have had little opportunity to improve her wealth or social status. However, she was clever, resourceful and good looking and had three husbands who left her their lands and money when they died. When she fell out with her fourth husband, George Talbot, the sixth Earl of Shrewsbury, she fought him through the courts for property and money. When he died she carried on the fight against his family for 17 years. She was one of the most powerful and wealthy women in England, becoming famous for the construction of many grand buildings.

Bess was an unusual woman in the sixteenth century, but she was not unique. Many women, of various different ranks in society, made successful and fulfilling lives for themselves.

The wives of traders and merchants would often help their husbands to run their businesses as well as running the household. If their husband died they might be able to keep the business – and their financial fortunes.

SOURCE Q

Alice Chester of Bristol continued her husband's trade importing iron from Spain. She did so well that she gave the city a loading crane for the docks and a fine carved wooden screen for one of the city churches.

An extract from a modern history textbook.

Women during wartime

In times of crisis, men often had to rely on the character and determination of their wives, who had to take life and death decisions for both themselves and their families. During the Civil War (1642–9) many women were left in charge of their households when their husbands went to fight. Sometimes they were attacked by the enemy and had to use their intelligence and resourcefulness to fight them off. Some even acted like army commanders, issuing orders to the servants on how to fight and negotiating truces when they could hold out no longer.

A number of women saw the Civil War as a chance to break out of the traditional role expected of them. Some became spies, others followed their husbands to war. Others even disguised themselves as men and fought in battles (see Source R).

An engraving showing a woman who disguised herself as a drummer boy in the Civil War. Her true identity was only discovered when she gave birth.

TASKS...

1 a) Complete your diagram or table by colouring or highlighting those things which you think meant that women's lives were dangerous.

   b) Use a second colour for those which indicate that women worked very hard.

   c) Use a third colour to show which ones tell us that women had minds of their own and could act independently.

2 Now, look at your diagram or table and try to make an assessment of women's lives in the sixteenth and seventeenth centuries. You could write a paragraph to summarise your assessment.

3 Think back to what you have learned about medieval medicine and childbirth. Can you identify any changes or improvements? Brainstorm your ideas in pairs.

Plenary

●──●

Women lived poor and miserable lives.

Women lived satisfying and happy lives.

Do you remember where you first placed sixteenth- and seventeenth-century women on the line? Now that you have finished this section, where do you stand on the line? Give three reasons or pieces of evidence which have changed or confirmed your decision. Explain why they are so important.

DID PEOPLE EAT A HEALTHY DIET?

Objectives

By the end of this section, you will understand:
- what the diets of rich and poor people were like
- how healthy the diets of the rich and poor were.

You will be able to:
- compare sets of evidence in order to draw a conclusion.

Starter

All of the foods below are eaten somewhere in the world and a lot of them are eaten in Britain. For example, pig's blood is the main ingredient of black pudding and sheep's stomach is used to make haggis.

cabbage   dog   dandelion leaves

horse

peacock   oysters   nettles   veal

peas   swan   lamb   cactus

pig's blood   rabbit   sheep's stomach   snails

Which foods in this list would you eat? Which ones would you not eat? Why? Share your views with a partner.

Which foods did people eat?

What we eat today depends on how we have been brought up, our culture and the country we live in, the food that is available and also what we can afford.

Many of the foods we take for granted were not available in the sixteenth and seventeenth centuries as transporting goods from other countries took a long time. Some countries had not yet been discovered by Europeans and so some foods we eat today were not known in Britain. (You will find out more about these 'undiscovered' countries in Chapter 12.) There was also no such thing as refrigeration, so fresh food would not keep for long.

TASKS...

1 In a group, try to work out which of the following would not normally have been available to people in England in 1500. Give your reasons.

apples	oysters	runner beans
cabbage	peacock	spinach
chocolate	pickled herrings	tea
coffee	pigeon	tomatoes
hare	pineapple	turkey
kangaroo	potatoes	venison
lemons	rice	

Daily bread and beer

Everyone ate a lot of bread at this time. Bread was baked daily and in a large household this would have kept some people fully employed. **Trenchers** of bread were provided for use as plates. For the very poorest people bread was necessary to keep them from starvation. When times were really hard and stocks of wheat or rye ran out, bread might have been made from beans or peas, or sometimes even from acorns.

People drank a lot of beer and ale. It was quite weak and much safer to drink than water.

💡 Why do you think that beer was safer to drink than water?

Key words

Trencher A platter or board for serving food.

An illustration from the 1598 _Ordinances of the York Bakers' Company_.

Storing food

As there was no refrigeration most food was kept in barrels. There was very little food for animals in the winter and so most animals would be slaughtered during the autumn. The meat would then be salted to stop it from rotting so that it could be eaten over the next few months. Wealthy people also preserved vegetables and fruit by salting, bottling and by making jams. The poor could rarely afford to do this.

TASKS...

1 Look at the statements below. They give details of people's diets and the effects these might have had on them.

Match up the causes with the consequences. The first one has been done for you. **WS**

CAUSES

1 When harvests failed poor people went hungry.

2 Breakfast for the rich was eaten in the bedroom – if it was eaten at all. Lunch was often several hours long and included as many as seven courses. Dinner might be a light snack or another lengthy meal.

3 Most animals had to be slaughtered in the autumn as there was little winter food for them. Meat was eaten quickly or salted down. By spring there was little meat left.

4 Poor people's most frequent meal was 'pottage' – thin vegetable soup.

5 Every Friday and during Lent fish had to be eaten instead of meat.

6 The rich ate a diet that was largely protein and fat.

7 Most poor people survived on coarse grey rye or barley bread.

8 The rich ate sweets and sugared pastries between meals.

9 Breakfast for the poor usually consisted of bread and weak ale. Lunch would be taken around 11 am. The main meal was eaten on return to the cottage at dusk.

CONSEQUENCES

A Fish is a good source of protein and essential minerals and fats but it was not always available away from the coast.

B Too much sugar leads to tooth decay.

C Over-eating causes obesity, which leads to heart disease and a range of other physical problems.

D Vegetables are an essential part of a balanced diet.

E Too much meat and fat makes people ill.

F Lack of food lowered resistance to disease.

G When there was enough food, the three meals were well spaced and not too heavy – a good balance.

H Grain milled with the husk provides a good source of fibre.

I Lack of protein, vitamins and minerals leads to malnutrition and a range of physical complaints.

How healthy were the meals of the rich and the poor?

Have you had a special meal recently – perhaps for a birthday, or even a wedding? What was on the menu? As you read the following sources, think about whether you would prefer your meal or whether you would have liked to feast in Tudor and Stuart style.

SOURCE B

Venison, lamb, pork, veal

Roast goose, duck, pheasant

Fruit pies, jellies of all colours in the shape of birds

Quince marmalade

Marzipan, sugarbread, gingerbread.

In Elizabeth I's reign, a well-off merchant served this meal to special guests.

SOURCE C

The table was served daily with 20 dishes at a course, three courses the year round. My lord was very curious in his wine, but Frontiniac was his favourite. He drank a whole quart (two bottles) at one go either of a malt drink or wine and water, having been advised by his doctor that it was a remedy for the **stone and gravel** which he was sometimes troubled with.

Sir Edward Southcote describes the food and drink at a large country house in 1660.

Key words

Quince A golden, pear-shaped fruit, often used for making jam.
Stone and gravel Kidney or bladder stones, a very painful condition.

SOURCE D

Breakfast	Bread and ale.
Mid-morning	Bread, cheese and ale.
Evening	Pottage: thin soup consisting of water and 'pot-herbs' (for example beans, peas, onions, nettles and other wild plants and herbs). In the autumn and winter there might be some meat.

A poor person's diet in the sixteenth century.

TASKS...

1 Who do you think was likely to have been healthier, the rich or the poor? There are arguments on both sides. Which do you think are the most persuasive? Remember, for both rich and poor diets:
   - write out all the good and bad points
   - use evidence to back up your points.

   When you have weighed up the arguments, decide which diet you think would have been healthier. Write this in a conclusion. Remember to use persuasive language and to give reasons for your decision. **WS**

2 Which diet would you prefer to have:
   a) A rich person's from the sixteenth century, or the special meal you described earlier?
   b) A poor person's diet from the sixteenth century, or the food you ate yesterday?

   Give reasons for your choice in each case. Discuss your ideas with someone else in your class.

3 In Tudor and Stuart times meals varied hugely according to the time of year. Make a list of reasons why this might be the case.

Plenary

Write out a shopping list for either a rich person or a poor person in the sixteenth century. Explain to someone else in your class why these items are on your list.

DID ELIZABETH I EFFECTIVELY TACKLE THE PROBLEM OF BEGGING?

WHY WERE PEOPLE POOR IN TUDOR TIMES?

Objectives

By the end of this section you will know:
- why people were poor in Tudor England
- why poverty increased in the mid-sixteenth century.

You will be able to:
- extract evidence from sources and classify this evidence.

Starter

Key words

Jags Dirty, ragged clothes.

> Hark, hark! The dogs do bark
>
> The beggars are coming to town.
>
> Some in rags and some in **jags**
>
> And one in a velvet gown.

This Tudor nursery rhyme gives the impression that beggars travelled round in groups from town to town and that not all of them were poor. Certainly Elizabeth I's government thought that beggars were a problem and laws were passed to deal with them.

Have you seen anyone begging in a large town or city? Discuss with a neighbour what your reactions to beggars are and why you feel that way.

- *What did you think of the person begging?*
- *Why do you think they were begging in this way?*

Do you think the reasons for begging have always been the same, or are there different reasons for begging today?

Why were so many people poor in Tudor times?

By the end of Elizabeth I's reign there were a lot of beggars. Some rich people said there were so many because the poor were lazy and would do anything to avoid work – even risk being hanged. Was this really the case?

In Tudor times there was only charity to rely on if you could not look after yourself. Unfortunately, charity could not help everyone who needed it. While Elizabeth was queen (1558–1603) the government became increasingly concerned with the problem of beggars. There was an ever-growing number of poor and unemployed people and they were beginning to cause difficulties.

Key words

Vagrant A tramp.
Black Death An outbreak of plague in the mid-fourteenth century which killed millions of people throughout Europe.

Elizabeth I's government was worried because gangs of beggars, or **vagrants**, were wandering the roads from town to town. They were tricking people out of their money, or simply stealing from them, as they went. There was no police force like we have today and so it was quite difficult to prevent crimes like these from taking place.

Changes in farming

Although the **Black Death** of the fourteenth century had resulted in the deaths of up to half the people in England, the population was beginning to rise again by the start of Elizabeth's reign in 1558. However, village life had changed forever. In the difficult times following the plague, landowners could not get enough labourers to work the land for them, so they had begun to rear more sheep, which needed less work than crops. One shepherd could look after a flock of sheep on his own but it took many people to harvest a field of wheat. For this reason landowners also started to enclose more land with fences and hedges. These enclosures meant that poor people could no longer use common land to rear their animals. Although the population was growing again, the number of jobs on the land was not.

John Spencer (a rich landowner) converted lands into pasture for sheep and other animals. Four persons who had been living and working there were made unemployed by this. They were driven into vagrancy.

An extract from a government report of 1517.

Sheep eat up and swallow crops. Men themselves – noblemen and gentlemen and certain abbots – leave no ground for crops, they enclose all into pastures. The labourer must be thrown out and soon what remains for them but to steal and be hung, or to wander about and beg?

Thomas More commented on the effects of enclosure in 1516.

A contemporary engraving showing a shepherd tending his flock in the late sixteenth century.

The cloth trade

Because more sheep were being reared, a great deal of money was being made from the cloth trade. This was England's biggest industry and a great deal of wool was sold abroad in Europe. Most villagers hoped to make some money during the year by spinning or weaving wool, and many merchants made their fortunes from cloth. However, when prices were low and the work of spinners and weavers was not wanted, many people became unemployed.

Rising prices

During Elizabeth's reign there were more people than there were jobs, so wages did not go up. This became a big problem because the price of goods was rising, so people could not afford to buy as much. This was made worse when there were poor harvests – and there were quite a few in the sixteenth century – because then the price of food also went up.

The loss of the monasteries

For centuries before Elizabeth I's reign, the Church had helped to deal with problems such as poverty and unemployment. Young men might train as priests or monks and so could be sure of having a living. Unmarried women with no male relative to support them could go into a convent and be secure for the rest of their lives. Monasteries also looked after the sick, helped travellers, educated young boys so they might do better in life and gave out charity to the very needy. After Henry VIII closed down the monasteries (see pages 16–20) this support for the poor and unemployed was lost.

Where could the poor turn for help?

Where did the poor and unemployed turn for support after the dissolution of the monasteries? If they had no relatives to help them, poor people might be forced to go into a poorhouse. Here they would be given food, shelter and work to do until they found a job of their own. However, people did not really want to do this – poorhouses were not very pleasant and anyway, there were not enough poorhouses to support all the poor and unemployed.

As people grew older they sometimes suffered from illnesses such as arthritis, which made it difficult for them to work. Often, the death of a husband left a widow with children to support and this could easily mean a life of poverty for the family.

SOURCE D

Anne Buckle is 46 years old and a widow. She has two children of 9 and 5, who make lace. They are very poor.

An extract from a report made in Norwich in 1570.

TASKS...

1 Colour each box in your spider diagram or mind map according to whether you think the reason for people's poverty was:

- *social (to do with their class and lifestyle)*
- *economic (to do with money)*
- *religious (to do with religion and the Church)*
- *political (to do with the big events happening in the country which were planned or dealt with by the government).*

Remember to include a key on your diagram. If you have time, you could illustrate your spider diagram with pictures to show why people were poor in the Tudor period.

2 **a)** *'You poor people ought to go out and find jobs instead of sitting around complaining that you're poor and begging from honest citizens like me. You're just lazy!'*

Compose your reply to this rich, Elizabethan gentleman.

Here is some advice to help you write a good speech:

First paragraph
Explain that there are a lot of reasons why you can't get a job. Write about what has happened over recent years to make people poor. You could include information about enclosures, prices and harvests.

Second paragraph
Explain why begging is your only option. Write about the help available for poor people – or the lack of it.

Third paragraph
Sum up your argument by explaining why the gentleman should change his attitude. Write about poor people's problems that are beyond their control such as illness and death. Show how the gentleman's class is partly to blame and say why he should take some responsibility for helping the poor.

b) When you have finished your response, swap your ideas with those of a partner. Compare your partner's plan with your own plan. Make a list of points they have left out.

c) Discuss whose plan has the most logical order of points to be made. Combine the best parts of both plans to produce a really good final speech.

Plenary

Read some of the speeches created by others in your class. Decide which speeches are the best and why. Discuss what makes a good speech. For example, what evidence has been used?

HOW DID THE DIFFERENT TYPES OF BEGGAR MAKE THEIR LIVING?

Objectives

By the end of this section you will know:
- what different types of beggar there were
- what *beggars' cant* was.

You will be able to:
- use beggars' cant to write a play or a conversation
- discuss the attitudes of beggars towards society, and of society towards beggars.

SOURCE A

A bright man Nicolas Blunt.

The counterfet Nicolas

Cranke Genynges

A seventeenth-century woodcut showing Nicholas Jennings, a famous beggar, in disguise as a 'cripple' and also as a gang leader.

Key words

Counterfeit Pretend, false.
Crank An ill person.

Starter

This woodcut shows two images of the same man, but wearing a different disguise.

How do you think he is trying to get money out of his victims?

*Nicholas Jennings was known as a '**Counterfeit Crank**'. One way in which he tried to get money from people was to pretend he was having an epileptic fit to get people's sympathy. He would use soap to make himself foam at the mouth – hence his other name of 'soap-sucker'.*

Why was begging such a problem during Elizabeth I's reign?

Brainstorm the answer to these questions:

- 💡 How do you know what is fashionable today?
- 💡 How do you know what the important issues are in the world?
- 💡 How would you find out whether there are any strikes happening, or whether it's going to be sunny tomorrow, or whether there's been a gruesome murder ten miles away?

Look at your answers to the questions above about accessing information. Very few of these sources of information were available in Tudor times. Most people were born, grew up, lived their lives and died in the same town or village. They found out about important events, and gossip, from going to church, talking to travellers and from their rare trips to market. This meant that people did not always know about the tricks that might be played on them by con-men and beggars.

Turning to a life of crime

As you learned from pages 115–9, people became poorer in Elizabeth I's reign. Some people turned to begging or a life of crime in order to make a living. Beggars tried to trick people into giving them money, or they might pretend to be someone they weren't in order to get an opportunity to steal. There were a number of recognisable types of beggar like the Counterfeit Crank. They had their own nicknames according to how they made their money. As you read about them, think about:

- 💡 Which were likely to be the most successful, and why?
- 💡 Which would be most dangerous for ordinary people to encounter?

A variety of con-men and beggars

The Abraham Man
He wore a sheet for clothing, with bare arms and legs, in order to look mad. He would often make strange noises, shouting out and staring wildly to add to the effect.

The Courtesy Man
He wore smart clothes and was well-spoken. He was very convincing and persuaded people to lend him money. He then disappeared without paying it back.

The Clapper Dudgeon
He put plants and salt on his body to make sores, then stuck cloth on to the sores to pull the flesh away. Then he would cover his body with dirty, bloody cloths. The Clapper Dudgeon travelled from market to market, often making five shillings a week (a good sum in those days). He sometimes had as much as six or seven pounds on him (more than most ordinary people would see in a year).

The Freshwater Mariner and Counterfeit Soldier or Ruffler
The Freshwater Mariner often appeared disabled, perhaps with a crutch, and claimed to have been wounded while fighting against the Spanish, usually for a famous sea captain such as Francis Drake. The Counterfeit Soldier would say he was a wounded war hero. He begged for food and money or used his sword to threaten people if they did not hand over their money.

The Rogue
He crawled along, supporting himself with a stick, dressed in tattered clothes and pretending to be weak and poor.

The Upright Man
Described as the 'king of vagrants', he did not lower himself to beg. He simply threatened people in order to get money, even taking it from other vagrants. He also took their women.

Women were not above begging either:

The Doxy

She carried all her stolen goods in a pack on her back, knitting as she went along. Her favourite trick was to feed chickens with bread attached to a hook and a thread. The chicken took the bread, choked and then she carried it off under her cloak.

The Dummerer

She made strange noises to indicate that her tongue had been cut out. Then she would put a sharp stick in her mouth as if to show her lack of tongue. Instead she would cut her tongue to make it bleed so that all that could be seen was blood.

The Bawdy Basket

She carried a basket, apparently selling lace, pins and coloured silk. She stole clothes when they were laid out to dry and talked maidservants into giving her food from their mistress's kitchen in exchange for small worthless pieces of jewellery.

Beggars' cant

These vagrants or vagabonds even had their own sort of slang to talk to each other so that ordinary people did not understand what they were saying. People have always used slang to their friends – people 'in the know' – who belong to their group, for example Cockney rhyming-slang. Fifty years ago a Londoner might have said:

'I put a pony on with the geezer but the nag came a cropper at the first'.

This means that he bet £25 with a man but the horse he put the money on fell at the first fence. Today slang is used which involves the kind of rap and street language that you might use with your friends. Beggars' cant was very much like this, as you can see from the chart below.

Beggars' cant	Meaning
maunding	begging
pannum	bread
stow you!	shut up!
peck	food
bring a waste!	get out of here!
cove	person, chap
boozing ken	pub
filch	stick
cloy	steal
mort	woman
duds	clothes
queer ken	prison
glaziers	eyes
darkmans	night
tip	give

TASKS...

1 In groups, write *either* a conversation between two beggars *or* a play in which some beggars from outside a village try to get money out of a local man. Decide which type of beggar they are (look at pages 122–3). When they talk to each other they will use beggars' cant. When they talk to non-beggars they will use normal English. Include some statements on why they have become beggars, whether they are successful or not and what non-beggars think of them.
Be prepared to perform the plays or read out the conversations. **WS**

Plenary

Look at the plays or conversations written by other groups. Try to work out the beggars' cant and explain what the beggars were saying to each other.

WERE THE LAWS TO DEAL WITH BEGGARS EFFECTIVE?

Objectives

By the end of this section you will understand:
- what laws were passed to deal with beggars
- why these laws were not effective
- what Elizabeth I's government did as a response to the situation
- the different views about the effectiveness of the Elizabethan Poor Law.

You will be able to:
- explain why the existing laws did not solve the problem of begging
- explain how the new Poor Law operated
- use sources to decide how the Poor Law has been interpreted.

Starter

'To stop begging, beggars should have been hanged for a first offence.'

'Beggars weren't to blame for their situation. The government should have given them money and homes.'

If these two extreme views appeared at each end of a line across the classroom, where would you stand on the line?

💡 *How would you justify your decision?*

In groups, discuss where people chose to stand.

💡 *Do a lot of people share similar views? Why do you think this is?*

Why was action on begging needed?

Elizabeth I's government was very concerned about the number of vagrants and vagabonds in England. It was an unsettled and dangerous time. There had been threats against Elizabeth's life, the Spanish had tried to invade England in 1588 and there were several plots to overthrow the government. Having a lot of discontented poor people roaming around the country, with no checks on their whereabouts or behaviour, was very worrying for the government.

The problems with beggars

- *There were a lot of beggars.*
- *A large number of beggars seemed to be tricksters and criminals.*
- *Some people were genuinely poor and unemployed.*
- *Beggars were difficult to catch because they moved round from place to place and there was no police force.*

Look at the problems. What might Elizabeth's ministers have done about each one? Discuss your ideas with a partner and make a list.

Who was responsible for the poor in Tudor times?

During Elizabeth's reign, each **parish** was responsible for its poor people. The nearest modern equivalent to the parish is a local council. The man in charge of the parish was the Justice of the Peace (JP). He was responsible for many things including dealing with petty criminals, seeing that the roads were repaired and looking after the poor. He was not paid. Neither was his chief assistant, the Constable, whose job was to enforce the JP's decisions and to catch criminals like vagabonds and thieves.

Key words

Parish The area around a church.

Everybody belonged to a parish. When you were born, your name would be entered into a big book called the Parish Record Book. The JP collected money from the rich people in the parish to take care of the poor. However, the number of poor people was growing during the Tudor period (see pages 116–9).

Why was it difficult to decide what to do about the poor in Tudor times?

What were the laws on begging and why weren't they working?

During the Tudor period begging was seen as a crime by the government. The government did not sympathise with the reasons people gave for becoming beggars. For this reason, a number of laws were passed about begging (see the timeline below).

LAWS ABOUT BEGGING

1531 Vagrants should be tied to a cart, stripped to the waist, and whipped through the streets. They should then be sent back to their home parish.

1547 Anyone unemployed for three days is a vagrant. He should be **branded** with a 'V' and made a slave of the person who reported him as being a vagrant. If he doesn't do everything his master asks, he can be whipped, imprisoned or executed.

1572 Vagrants should be whipped and have a hole bored through their ear. For a third offence they may be executed.

Key words

Branded Burnt with a hot iron. Branding was a common punishment. Thieves were branded with the letter 'T' on their forehead.

TASKS...

1 From what you have learned so far about beggars and the difficulties of life in Elizabethan England, can you think of six reasons why the three laws on begging had little impact on the problem?
List these and share them with a partner.

TASKS...

2 How might some of the laws passed to stop begging actually have caused more begging?

a) Match up what the laws said with the reasons they failed. The first one has been done for you.

WHAT THE LAWS SAID

1	*Vagrants could be branded with a 'V'.*
2	*Vagrants should have a hole bored through their ear.*
3	*Anyone unemployed for three days was a vagrant.*
4	*Vagrants should be whipped and sent back to their home parish.*
5	*For a third offence a beggar could be executed.*
6	*A vagrant could be made a slave of the person who reported him.*

REASONS FOR FAILURE

A	*Beggars often left their home parish because there was no work. Sending them back would not help them to get a job.*
B	*The person who owned the slave might not be able to afford to feed him and the slave might be treated badly.*
C	*This was very drastic. JPs were reluctant to have a man hanged simply for begging so they ignored this law.*
D	*There was a great deal of unemployment. If he was going to be classed as a vagrant, a man might as well beg and try to make some money.*
E	*Who would give a branded man a job?*
F	*This could be hidden with long hair or an earring.*

b) Which reasons for continued begging are not even dealt with by the laws? Make a list.

c) Discuss with a partner why the government might not have addressed these problems.

3 Where would you want to put yourself on the line below? Have you changed your mind having read this section? You should justify your decision by using what you have learned about begging in Elizabethan England.

●─────────────────────────────────────●

'To stop begging, beggars should have been hanged for a first offence.'

'Beggars weren't to blame for their situation. The government should have given them money and homes.'

What did the Elizabethan government do about the problem of begging?

As you have discovered, the three laws on begging (see page 127) were not working. So Elizabeth's government passed more laws, in 1598 and 1601. These laws, called Poor Laws, said that there were two different types of poor people.

> **Deserving Poor** – those who could not work or were poor through no fault of their own, for example widows with young children or the disabled.

> **Idle Poor** – people who were 'able-bodied' (fit and healthy) but who avoided work through laziness or dishonesty.

 Do you think that dividing poor people in this way would have been a step forward, or not? Why?

The two types of poor people were to be treated differently. Clearly, the deserving poor were not a threat to the government.

The deserving poor

- Each parish is to appoint two 'overseers of the poor'. They will make sure that money is collected from the rich to help the deserving poor. This money is called the poor rate.
- Only those people on the Parish Register can receive help.
- Each parish is to build a poorhouse for the poor and sick. In the poorhouse the poor will receive help. This is known as 'indoor relief'. Basic work will also be provided in the poorhouse, to help pay for the system.
- If there is no poorhouse in a parish, then the poor will be helped in their own homes. This is to be known as 'outdoor relief'.
- **Pauper** children will be sent to a craftsman to learn a trade (such as carpentry) as soon as they are old enough.

The idle poor

- Vagrants are to be whipped until bloody and sent back to the parish where they were born.
- Vagrants who are able-bodied are to be made to work.
- If vagrants continue to beg they will be put in a House of Correction (rather like a prison) or hanged.

Key words

Pauper A poor person.

A seventeenth-century illustration of a beggar being whipped through the streets.

In 1601 the government passed a new Poor Law. It lasted for two hundred years. It was a great success.

An extract from a modern history textbook.

SOURCE Ⓒ

It was hoped that harsh punishment would frighten people into obeying the law, but since there was so little chance of getting caught, crime continued to flourish.

An extract from a history textbook, published in 2000.

SOURCE Ⓓ

This was the first time that the Crown and the ruling classes had organised proper help for the poor. The system lasted until the nineteenth century; it was not perfect and poverty did not disappear, but it was a start.

An extract from a modern history textbook.

TASKS...

1 Imagine you are a well-off member of society in 1601. Write a formal letter to your local newspaper explaining why you think that the Poor Law is a good or a bad idea. Make sure you say who you are and how you will be affected by the new law. You should also make some comments about the following:

- The cost – is it fair that the rich are to pay for the poor?

- The organisation (overseers/poorhouses) – do you think it is a good idea to have special buildings for poor people?
- Justices of the Peace – will they be able to cope with the extra work?
- Houses of Correction – will they persuade beggars to stop living a life of crime?
- Jobs for the able-bodied – are there enough? How can poor people support themselves otherwise?

TASKS...

2 What do Sources B–D tell us about the effect the Poor Laws had on crime and poverty?

3 Does the fact that the Poor Laws lasted until 1834 mean that they were effective?

Plenary

Look at these groups of words. For each group, choose one that is the odd one out. Be prepared to justify your choices!

Group A	1 deserving poor	2 idle poor	3 paupers
Group B	1 poorhouse	2 indoor relief	3 outdoor relief
Group C	1 unemployment	2 vagrancy	3 illness

Now try to create your own group of words with an odd one out. Try your groups on a partner.

8

DID CRIME PAY IN THE SIXTEENTH AND SEVENTEENTH CENTURIES?
HOW WAS CRIME DEALT WITH?

Starter

Make a list of common crimes and punishments in Britain today.

Discuss the following questions in a group and share your ideas:

- *What are the most serious crimes?*
- *What are the most severe punishments?*
- *What is the purpose of punishment?*

Why was torture used in the sixteenth century?

Five hundred years ago life was much harder for people than it is today. Death was an everyday event:
- more children died than survived
- many women died in childbirth
- wounds often went bad causing blood poisoning and death
- many diseases were fatal.

Punishments were also harsher than they are today:
- thieves might be hanged for their crimes
- queens were beheaded for adultery
- heretics were burned at the stake.

People accepted the idea of pain and suffering, so it was not surprising that pain was inflicted on prisoners for a variety of reasons. Although torture could only be used at the command of the monarch, there was more torture used in England in the Tudor period than at any other time before or since.

💡 Why do you think that people in the sixteenth century thought that the use of torture was justified?

SOURCE A

An illustration of the execution of Edmund Campion, a missionary who was caught in England promoting Catholicism. He was hanged, drawn and quartered in 1581.

SOURCE B

A contemporary drawing of Cuthbert Simson on the rack. Simson was a Protestant who was tortured in the last year of Queen Mary's reign.

SOURCE C

His nails on all his fingers were torn and under every nail two needles were thrust in.

King James I believed in witchcraft and accused a certain Dr Fain of causing a storm to try to wreck his ship on a sea voyage. This was one method used to get Dr Fain to confess.

SOURCE D

In 1605 a group of Catholics planned to blow up King James I and Parliament. The first conspirator to be caught, Guy Fawkes, was discovered in a cellar below the Houses of Parliament. He was questioned by the king and then tortured for information.

An extract from a modern history textbook.

1   Write a paragraph to answer the question:
    Why was torture used by the authorities in the sixteenth century?

2   Can you think of any reasons why torture would not be a good method
    for getting accurate information from the victim? Explain your answer.

How were criminals punished?

In the sixteenth century some prisoners were sentenced to very
painful deaths. Today we would probably regard these punishments
as forms of torture. People accepted that punishment meant
suffering, but not all criminals were treated equally.

A quick way to die was by having your head chopped off, but this
form of execution was used only for people of noble birth. The
traditional punishment for traitors was execution by hanging,
drawing and quartering. The condemned men would be hanged until
nearly suffocated but were cut down before they died. Next they
would be castrated, disembowelled and their bowels burnt before
their eyes. Finally they were cut into four pieces which were then
fixed on poles around the city.

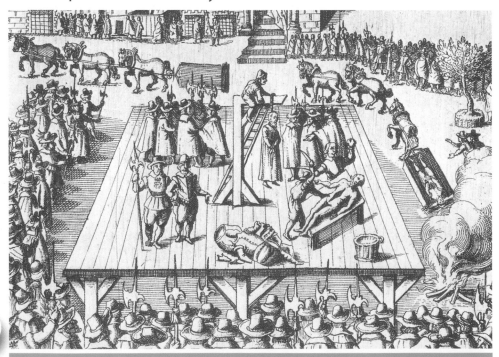

The execution of four traitors by hanging, drawing
and quartering, from a print published at the time.

The execution of traitors, like the burning of heretics, took place in public. The traitors were brought to Tyburn from prison tied face downward on a hurdle drawn by horses. As with burning, how much and how long they suffered varied in every case. The traitor or his family usually paid money to the executioner to allow the traitor, against the sentence of the court, to hang until he was dead, or to kill him quickly with a knife as soon as he was cut down and before his bowels were cut out. If the executioner was not paid enough, or wanted the condemned man to suffer, he might deliberately prolong the execution.

An account of Tudor punishment from a modern history textbook.

SOURCE G

Noblemen were the only prisoners who were allowed to be beheaded, and they were executed on Tower Hill. They were allowed to walk the few yards to Tower Hill instead of being drawn there on a hurdle. They usually gave a small gift to the executioner, to encourage him to do his job well and quickly. Sometimes the victim died at the first stroke of the axe, but sometimes two or three strokes were necessary.

Another common form of punishment was whipping. Offenders were sometimes sentenced to be whipped through the streets when tied behind a slow-moving cart. Offenders were also placed in the stocks where they were forced to sit fastened by the legs, or to stand in the pillory. They were surrounded by crowds who pelted them with eggs, stones and rotting meat. Sentences of mutilation were also imposed. The criminal was sentenced to have an ear nailed to the pillory or cut off. Various laws were passed stating that certain offences were to be punished by cutting off the offender's hand.

An extract from a modern textbook.

A drawing from 1613, showing two people being punished in the pillory for pretending to be fortune tellers.

Key words

Plead To say whether you are innocent or guilty when you are on trial.

Peine forte et dure A French phrase meaning 'strong and hard pain'.

Unconvicted Not found guilty.

If a person accused of a crime refused to **plead**, he could not be found guilty and so his estates would not be taken by the government. The penalty for this, however, was **'peine forte et dure'**. The victim would be laid down on the floor of his prison cell, then weights would be piled upon him until he died.

On 23 April 1605, Walter Calverley, in a fit of jealous and drunken madness, killed his two sons and his wife. He intended to kill a surviving son, Henry, but was arrested before he could do so. Imprisoned at York Castle, Calverley refused to plead so that Henry could inherit his goods and estate. In August, Calverley was pressed to death, an **unconvicted** man.

In 1672 at the Monmouth court, Henry Jones refused to plead and was sentenced to be pressed. His agony began on Saturday, the day after he appeared in court, and he did not die until midday on Monday.

An extract from a modern book on punishment and torture.

TASKS...

1 Look at Sources E to I. Why do you think so many Tudor punishments were carried out in public?

2 You are a Tudor judge in the reign of Elizabeth I. Decide what punishments you might have given if the following people were sentenced in your court.
Study Sources E to I to help you make your decisions:

  a) A lord who had plotted to assassinate Elizabeth I.

  b) A Catholic missionary who was found in hiding.

  c) A labourer who stole from a shop.

  d) An unemployed woman who tricked a servant into giving her some of her mistress's silver.

  e) A shopkeeper who refused to plead when accused of murdering his wife.

Read your decisions to the court (the rest of the class) explaining why your decision is appropriate.

Plenary

Write down three questions about torture and punishment that you have answered in this section and three questions you have not answered. Where and how might you find the answers to the last three questions?

WHY DID CRIME INCREASE IN THE SIXTEENTH AND SEVENTEENTH CENTURIES?

Objectives

By the end of this section you will know:
- why there was so much crime in towns
- what types of crime were common in the Tudor period.

You will be able to:
- complete an activity using evidence from sources
- use historical evidence to tell a story
- practise the literacy skills of news reporting.

A homeless person begging in modern-day Europe.

A person begging in the seventeenth century.

Starter

💡 *Do you think that begging, as shown in Source A, should be a crime?*

💡 *Why might the man have ended up begging?*

💡 *What do you think might happen to him in the future?*

💡 *Do you think that the beggar in Source B should have been treated as a criminal?*

💡 *Why might he have ended up begging?*

💡 *What do you think might have happened to him next?*

Why was there so much crime in towns?

TASKS...

1 Which of the following do you think would have been most important in causing the high crime rate in Elizabethan England? Put them in order of importance from the most important to the least important. Be prepared to give reasons for your decisions.

Enclosures put many people out of work.

Towns were growing quickly.

When the man of the house was ill or died, the rest of the family was often faced with poverty.

There weren't enough jobs to go round.

There was no street lighting in towns or villages.

There was only one constable per parish.

Cruelty to apprentices meant that up to 50 per cent of them ran away.

There was no organised police force.

2 Can you think of any other reasons why people might have turned to crime? Make a list and again put your reasons in order of importance.

3 As you read the next section, make a list of the crimes mentioned.

What types of crime existed?

As you have already seen, Elizabeth I's government was so worried about the problem of beggars and vagabonds that it introduced new laws (the Poor Laws of 1598 and 1601) to deal with them. What beggars were actually doing was stealing – they tricked people to get their money. However, beggars were only part of the problem in Elizabethan England. As towns grew in size, so the crime rate also rose.

Begging was one way in which people could make a living by taking other people's money. Large towns also had pickpockets, burglars and cut-purses – who would steal a man's purse by cutting it from his belt. There were also confidence-tricksters – people who persuaded their victims to hand over money by getting them to trust them. Gangs of ex-soldiers even used weapons to hold people up and rob them. Some shopkeepers used faulty weights to give their customers short measures.

A respectably dressed traveller asked for a room and food and drink; he asked for the largest silver bowl in the inn to be filled with drink, lemons and sugar, with a silver spoon to stir it, under the pretence of having it by him in his own room all night. In the dead of night he got up, took his horse out of the stable, put straw on the ground so that no-one would hear his horse and took away the bowl, spoon, pillow, beer and bed linen, valued at £15.00.

A description of a burglary written in 1691.

Three months ago I caught a thief – who was later executed. He confessed to me that he and two others stayed in an alehouse for three weeks. During this time they ate twenty fat sheep, which they stole one a night. They also ruined many a poor man's ploughing by stealing an ox from him.

A Justice of the Peace in Elizabeth I's reign describes the activities of robbers.

Shoplifting became a more frequent crime even though the punishment for stealing more than five shillings (25p) was hanging. In coastal towns there was smuggling as well. London had so many criminals they even had their own part of the city, which they called Alsatia.

There were also many crimes of violence and fighting was common. Fights could break out perhaps because of a dispute between gentlemen over an accusation of cheating at cards, or because of a general brawl among apprentices.

The most serious crimes were murder and treason – plotting against the government. Anyone involved in plotting to overthrow the monarch or to challenge the government by force could expect little mercy if they were caught.

A drawing of the highwayman William Davis robbing a tinker in 1664.

SOURCE F

There has been a complaint about a dog belonging to Peter Quotes, which offends the neighbours and will steal out of their houses whole pieces of meat like loins of mutton and veal. The dog will not spoil it but carries it whole to his master's house. This is a profitable dog for his master, but because he is offensive to many it is not to be suffered, so his master is fined three shillings and fourpence for every time.

An entry from the Southampton Court Records.

The popular press

The invention of the printing press led eventually to books and pamphlets being produced on subjects other than religion. Pamphlets were the Tudor equivalent to news reports on television or in newspapers. Stories about crime and punishment proved especially popular during the sixteenth and seventeenth centuries.

TASKS...

1 Compare your list of crimes with your neighbour's and add any you missed to your list.
2 Rank the crimes from the most serious to the least serious.
3 On what basis did you decide whether a crime was serious?
4 What punishment do you think should have gone with each crime?

SOURCE G

A seventeenth-century pamphlet showing execution by hanging.

TASKS...

1 Produce a news report about a crime and its punishment in Tudor England. You can make an Elizabethan pamphlet like the one in Source G on page 140, or you can create a modern equivalent like the ones we see today. Choose from: **WS**

- a television documentary on a criminal's life
- a newspaper report on a sensational crime
- a policeman's evidence in court
- a criminal's deathbed confession
- evidence presented in court, for which you have to decide if the accused is guilty or innocent.

Use what you have learned so far to get ideas for your report. You will also need to think about:

- Who was the criminal?
- What sort of crime was committed?
- How was the crime carried out?
- How was the criminal caught?
- How was the criminal punished?
- How you can make your story interesting while still keeping it realistic.

2 You have now gathered enough information to be able to answer the big question at the beginning of this chapter:
'Did crime pay in the sixteenth and seventeenth centuries?' **WS**
Before you start your answer, make notes to answer the short questions which follow. Then use these notes to help you in your answer to the big question.

- What crimes were people able to get away with easily?
- How were they able to get away with these crimes?
- If they were caught, how were they punished?
- What did people consider the most serious crimes?
- If someone was charged with a serious crime, what might the punishment be?

3 Do you think that Tudor society was more violent than ours today? Why? Give reasons for your answers.

Plenary

In small groups, talk for 60 seconds on 'Crime in the sixteenth century'. If you hesitate, go off the subject or repeat key words, someone else will take over. The person speaking at the end of the minute is the winner.

9

WHY WAS THERE A WITCH-CRAZE IN THE SEVENTEENTH CENTURY?

WHY DID PEOPLE BELIEVE IN WITCHES?

Objectives

By the end of this section you will know:
- why many people were afraid of witches in the sixteenth and seventeenth centuries
- what events were linked to witchcraft.

You will be able to:
- link the fear of witchcraft with ideas, superstitions and lack of knowledge.

Starter

A modern artist's impression of the trial of Tracy Smith.

The scene above shows a modern courtroom. A woman, Tracy Smith, is on trial accused of offences against her neighbour. The lawyer for the prosecution is summing up his evidence for the jury.

SOURCE A

Read Source A.

If you were a member of the jury, would you believe that Tracy Smith was responsible for the things that had happened to Sarah Wilson? Why?

Make a list of the evidence you considered before coming to your conclusion, for example Tracy Smith had rat poison and Sarah Wilson's cat had been poisoned.

Now compare your list with your neighbour's and discuss any differences and the reasons for them.

The defendant, Tracy Smith, was a neighbour of the victim, Sarah Wilson, and often used to baby-sit for her. One day they quarrelled. Tracy had asked to borrow some money and Sarah had refused to lend it to her. A witness stated that Tracy was very angry and shouted 'I'll get you for that'. From that moment, Sarah started to notice things going wrong. She went out one morning to find that her car had been badly scratched. Rubbish began appearing in her garden. Her cat was poisoned. She received anonymous threatening telephone calls from a female with the same accent as Tracy Smith's. Police evidence shows that these calls came from a public telephone at the end of Tracy Smith's street. Tracy cannot account for her movements at the time when these calls were made. Her fingerprints were also found on the door of Sarah's car and a box of rat poison was found in her garage.

I suggest to you, members of the jury, that Tracy Smith has carried out a vicious campaign of harassment against Sarah Wilson. You should find her guilty.

The prosecution sums up its evidence for the jury.

Why did people believe that witchcraft was the cause of bad things which happened to them?

In Scotland at the end of the sixteenth century and in England in the mid-seventeenth century there was a witch-craze. Thousands of people were executed for practising 'witchcrafts, enchantments, charms and sorceries'. What caused people to believe in witchcraft and that witches could do them serious harm?

TASKS...

1   As you read the information which follows, make a list of the reasons why people believed in witches. Highlight your reasons with different colours to show which of the reasons are based on:

● fear and superstition
● religion
● lack of knowledge.

You could highlight some in more than one colour.

Wise women, or witches?

By 1500 people had believed in witches for centuries. In small villages little was known about health or medicine. It was taken for granted that there would be people – usually old women – who were skilled in using herbs to make medicines and other potions. They often helped when someone was ill or having a baby and they were usually referred to as 'wise women'.

Unexplained events

Sometimes people living on their own appeared odd – perhaps they talked to their animals – and occasionally people made fun of them or argued with them. In every village there were events for which people could not see a cause, like cattle dying and babies suffering from fits. Dangerous diseases like smallpox were not understood and people did not know how to prevent or cure them.

In general, people did not understand very much about how the natural world worked. Neither did they understand mental illness, which frightened people. This meant that anyone who acted in a strange way was looked on with suspicion. People thought that they might be 'possessed' by evil spirits.

The role of religion

As you discovered in Chapters 1, 2 and 4, the sixteenth and seventeenth centuries were a time of great religious belief. When people went to church they were told about the evil ways of the devil and the horrors of hell. Plagues like the Black Death were blamed on people's wickedness. It was thought that God had sent a punishment or that the Devil was to blame.

💡 Why do you think people were so frightened of witches?

TASKS...

1 Study the following evidence about accusations of witchcraft.

  a) As you read the sources, make a table showing all the events which were blamed on witchcraft. Write these on the left-hand side of the table.

  b) Opposite each event, on the right-hand side of the table, write any possible natural or scientific explanations you can think of for what happened.

  c) Highlight the explanations that people in the seventeenth century would probably not know about. Use the colour you have already used for 'lack of knowledge'.

SOURCE B

Sometimes they would limp on one side of their bodies, sometimes on the other. Sometimes they would be sore over their whole bodies, so they couldn't bear anyone to touch them. At other times they would be able to use their limbs perfectly but couldn't hear. At other times they couldn't see or speak. At other times they would faint, sometimes they would cough and bring up a lot of phlegm containing crooked pins. Once they coughed up a nail with a very broad head. The pins, amounting to forty or more, together with the nail were produced in court.

Amy Duny was accused of bewitching 11-year-old Elizabeth Pacy and her sister. This is an account of what was said at Amy's trial in 1645.

SOURCE C

She confessed that the devil appeared to her in the shape of a little dog. She said it told her to leave God and lean towards him ...; She called her devil by the name of Bunnie. Bunnie carried Thomas Gardler out of a window, and he fell into a cesspool. She gave some of her blood to the Devil. She said that Jane Holt, Elizabeth Harris and Joan Argoll were her partners. Her devil told her that Elizabeth Harris cursed the boat of John Woofcott.

Joan Williford's confession in 1645 was enough for her to be sentenced to death.

SOURCE D

She said that Isabel asked her for some milk but she refused. Afterwards she met Isabel and was afraid of her. She was then sick and hurting so much she could not stand. The next day, going to Warrington, she was suddenly pinched on her thigh with four fingers and a thumb. She was instantly sick – so much so that she couldn't walk home and had to go on horseback. Soon after she got better.

Jane Wilkinson's evidence against Isabel Robey, given at a trial of witches in Lancaster in 1612.

SOURCE E

It was not just poor, uneducated and superstitious villagers who believed in witchcraft. The highest people in the land also believed in it, and they were not afraid of telling people!

- Henry IV accused his step-mother of making him ill.
- King Richard III accused a woman of taking part in a plot to overthrow him by using witchcraft.
- Henry VIII accused Anne Boleyn of bewitching him into marrying her.

- James I accused a woman of causing a storm in order to wreck his ship. He was so concerned about witchcraft that he wrote a book about it called 'Demonology'. He had a law passed in 1604 which said that witches could be hanged.
- Elizabeth I had a law passed which said murder by witchcraft was punishable by death.

If the rulers of the country believed in the power of witchcraft, then ordinary people were likely to believe in it too.

A modern historian writing about witchcraft.

SOURCE F

Witches were charged with causing all sorts of unpleasant things to happen. When animals got diseases or died, when people had accidents or died unexpectedly, when their beer went off or their butter wouldn't churn, or they had strange pains, or their crops failed, they would blame it on witchcraft. If there were hailstorms, or ships were wrecked, or babies had fits, illnesses or died, or if children behaved oddly or said strange things, or marks appeared on their bodies – it could be witchcraft.

An extract from a modern history book.

TASKS...

1 Produce a poster warning people how to identify signs of witchcraft. Remember that not many people could read at the time so your poster should be largely visual – try to use as few words as possible. **WS**

Plenary

Write no more than 15 words to summarise the important things you have learned so far about why people believed in witchcraft. See whether your neighbour thinks the same things are important.

Discuss your ideas in a group and bullet point the five most important facts or ideas.

HOW WERE WITCHES IDENTIFIED?

Objectives

By the end of this section you will understand:
- how people identified witches
- the types of behaviour people linked with witchcraft.

You will be able to:
- extract information from a variety of sources to produce a stereotypical view.

Starter

Look at the cartoon of the witch. Write down everything you can see in this picture which tells you that the person shown is a witch. Discuss with a neighbour the reasons you came to your decisions.

A modern cartoon of a stereotypical witch.

Key words

Stereotypical A view of someone or something which relies on a common assumption, for example, Frenchmen wear striped jumpers and berets.

What did people think a witch was like?

During the sixteenth and seventeenth centuries a number of people wrote books on how witches might be recognised. Although there were some differences in what they wrote, most people agreed on how it was possible to identify a witch.

💡 As you read the following descriptions of witches, list the things that you think would tell you whether a person was a witch.

Witches are aged, with weak brains. They are very depressed and the devil takes advantage of this and tricks them into believing they have made a pact with him, making them think that they may do strange things. Our witches are wise and clever, crafty and cunning. Educated men have shown that all witches in Europe have similar behaviour and attitudes. They use the same answers, defences and protests.

A description of witches in the early seventeenth century by William Perkins, a Cambridge preacher.

Familiars – or imps or demons as they were sometimes known – were thought to be evil spirits that belonged to the witch and helped her to bewitch people. Familiars usually took the form of animals. Old people, who had little physical contact with other people, often turned to pets for companionship.

This drawing of witches with their familiars was made after the Chelmsford witch trials of 1589.

Key words

Aconite A poisonous medicinal plant.
Belladonna Deadly nightshade, also used in the preparation of medicines.

It was well known that witches had a range of supernatural abilities:

- They could make storms or huge waves, or cause plagues or crops to fail. People could not explain these things scientifically.
- They could fly on broomsticks. Old women often made their own ointments.

Preparations containing **aconite** or **belladonna** can give a feeling of rising up.

- They enjoyed sex. The Church preached that celibacy (not having sex) was a good thing.
- They could go to sea in a sieve: obviously this required serious magic!

A modern historian.

A seventeenth-century pamphlet about a witch.

How did people know so much about witches?

In the seventeenth century the printing press was beginning to make information available to people. Stories and drawings could be bought cheaply. Although many people were still **illiterate**, there was a big market for mysteries and horror just like today. Tales of witch trials were very popular and so pamphlets were produced, giving details of the accusations, trials and punishment of witches (see Source D).

Key words

Illiterate Unable to read.

TASKS...

1 Imagine that you are a printer in 1645. People want to know about the witches who have been caught in Essex. Printing these stories can make you money.

 a) Produce a pamphlet about a witch trial in 1645. You want to make it as interesting as possible by including a lot of information. **WS**
  • Start by designing the front page.

  • Draw and describe the witch using the information about what witches looked like and how they acted.
  • Give specific details of the charges and evidence brought against the witch.

 b) As you learn more about witchcraft in the seventeenth century, add more information to your pamphlet.

Plenary

Show the front page of your pamphlet to your group and explain the characteristics of witches you have tried to show in your picture. What did you have to describe in words rather than pictures?

WHY WERE WITCHFINDERS SO ACTIVE IN ENGLAND IN THE 1640s?

Objectives

By the end of this section you will find out:
- why witchfinders were invited to villages to seek out witches
- what encouraged the fear of witches
- that witchfinders caused hundreds of women to be hanged for witchcraft
- how witchfinders caused people to confess to witchcraft.

You will be able to:
- explain how some problems in society encouraged people to believe in witches
- produce an information pamphlet using evidence from sources.

Starter

In groups, take turns to list the reasons why someone might be suspected of witchcraft. Before you add your reason, you must repeat what everybody else has said. For example, 'A woman might be suspected of witchcraft because someone's cows had died'. 'A woman might be suspected of witchcraft because someone's cows had died and because people were afraid of the Devil', and so on. How many reasons can your group remember?

Why was there so much concern about witchcraft in England in the 1640s?

TASKS...

1. Look at the nine events and facts listed at the top of page 151. Which of them do you think would have given people reason to believe that witches were at work in the 1640s? List them in order of importance, from the most important to the least important. **WS**
   Be prepared to justify your decisions.

2. Compare your order of importance with others in the class. Discuss the list until you have decided on the five most important reasons.

The upheaval of the Civil War had made people scared and uncertain.	It was difficult to get news and information in country areas.	People were poorer – villages had lost crops and workers in the Civil War.
England had become Protestant. Catholicism had seemed to offer protection against the devil and sorcery.	People were confused about what was happening to their world.	The government was a long way away in London. It kept changing and no-one knew what was happening.
In the new Protestant Church the priest didn't have special powers to protect people – he was just an ordinary man.	Puritans believed that people had to be constantly on the alert against evil and the works of the devil.	Country people were very superstitious.

Why did people invite witchfinders to their village?

Witchfinders presented themselves to villagers as official people, supported by the highest authorities. In fact they set themselves up as experts without official approval and they gained people's trust by claiming that they could discover witches.

Matthew Hopkins, often called the Witchfinder General, began his career by making a one-legged woman called Elizabeth Clarke confess to being a witch. Hopkins and his assistants kept her awake for three days until she eventually confessed and named another five witches. Hopkins went on to make a career of ridding local communities in East Anglia of witches.

The belief that there were so many witches in their area must have been frightening for the local people.

Matthew Hopkins Witch Finder Generall

My Imps names are

Holt

1 Ilemauzar
2 Pyewackett

Jarmara

Sacke
& Sugar

3 Pecke in the Crowne
4 Griezzell Greedigutt

Newes

Vinegar Tom

A seventeenth-century illustration showing Matthew Hopkins and Elizabeth Clarke (drawn twice) with her familiars.

💡 Which parts of Source A do you think would have interested or concerned people at the time? Why?

💡 Do you think that Source A shows what really happened? Why?

💡 If Source A is not a true reflection of the facts, how can it still be a useful piece of evidence for historians?

SOURCE Ⓑ

Greetings, your Worship,

I have received a letter to come to your town to search for evil people, called witches. But I hear your minister is against us, through ignorance. I will come (God willing) to hear his views. I have heard a minister in Suffolk speak against the discovery of witches but he was soon forced to change his mind. I shall visit your town soon. I would like first to know whether I will get a good reception. If not, I shall go instead where people will accept me with thanks and payment.

Your servant,

Matthew Hopkins

A letter written in 1645 by Hopkins to the magistrate of a town in Essex.

TASKS...

1 a) According to Source B, some Protestant ministers were opposed to the activities of witchfinders. The minister of this town had obviously stated his views about witchfinders. What do you think he said?

b) Write the speech this minister might have made to his congregation in church explaining why Hopkins should not be invited to the village. Use the information you have learnt about why the 1640s were such an uncertain time for people. How might this have encouraged a belief in witches? **WS**

Why were witchfinders so successful?

TASKS...

1 Using information from Sources C to H, make a list of the methods witchfinders used to get confessions. Explain why each one would work.

2 When you have finished, look at the pamphlet you started about a witchcraft trial. Add a description of how the witchfinder got his evidence about the witch.

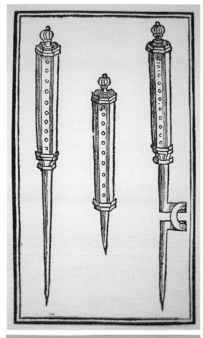

Tools used by a witchfinder.

💡 *What do you think the objects in Source C are used for? Write down possible answers.*

SOURCE D

The witchfinder would keep his victims awake, without food or sleep, until they would admit anything. The victim would usually be naked. Strapped to a stool she would suffer in agony, until her pets came from her home having sniffed their way there. This would be proof. It showed that they were in fact her imps who had come to their mistress. The victim would be flung into the water, left hand tied to right foot, right hand tied to left foot, and left to God's judgement. To float was a sure sign that you worked for the Devil, while to sink was to prove your innocence.

A historian, writing in 1981, describes the practices of sleep-deprivation and 'swimming' the victim used by witchfinders.

SOURCE E

I have heard that they kept him awake for several nights, and ran him backwards and forwards about the room until he was out of breath. Then they rested him a little and then ran him again. They did this for several days and nights until he was scarcely aware of what he said or did. They swam him at Framlingham but that was no true test to try him by; for they put in honest people at the same time and they swam as well as he did.

A report of the treatment of John Lowes, a Suffolk vicar, who was tried for witchcraft at Bury St Edmunds in 1615.

Witches Apprehended, Examined and Executed, for notable villanies by them committed both by Land and Water.

With a strange and most true triall how to know whether a woman be a Witch or not.

Printed at London for *Edward Marchant*, and are to

A pamphlet showing the practice of 'swimming' a witch.

A bishop told how one old woman was forced into confessing that she had an imp (a familiar) called Nan. She didn't know what she had confessed and only had a chicken that she sometimes called Nan. My opinion is that when the witchfinders had kept the poor people without food or sleep they didn't know what they said, then to stop the torture they told tales of their dogs and cats and kittens.

This view of the practices of witchfinder Matthew Hopkins was given in 1645.

When people began to have doubts about Hopkins' methods and honesty, he wrote a pamphlet called *The Discovery of Witches* to justify what he did, answering some of the questions usually put to him (see Source H).

Query: Once the Devil's mark has been discovered, why must the suspects be tortured and kept from sleep which will distract them and make them say anything?

Answer: It was thought best to do this, because if they were kept awake they would call their familiars to help them, which often happened.

Query: Beside keeping them awake, why did you force them to keep walking up and down until their feet were blistered and they confessed?

Answer: They were only walked to keep them awake. If they were allowed to sit or lie down, then their familiars came. This scared the guards and cheered the witches up.

Query: Why has 'swimming' been used? Throwing them into the water is inhumane and illegal.

Answer: King James said in his book *Demonology* that this was a sure test for a witch. Many ministers (whom I respect) have condemned swimming, so it is no longer done.

An extract from *The Discovery of Witches*, written by Matthew Hopkins in 1647.

How were convicted witches punished?

Hopkins may have been involved in the trials of about 200 women between 1645 and 1647. About half were sentenced to hang. Hopkins' reign of terror ended in 1647. After this time he seems to have disappeared and may have died that year.

In the eighteenth century, fewer people were executed for witchcraft. Instead 'witches' were sometimes imprisoned or put in the pillory.

TASKS...

1 Using the information you have read in this section, complete your pamphlet giving details of the fate of the witches. Don't forget to include information on anyone who was not found guilty.
The objects in Source C on page 153 are 'witchpricker's knives'. They were used to prick the skin of the person accused of being a witch in order to find a special mark showing where familiars sucked blood.

You could illustrate your pamphlet with a drawing like this.

2 Swap pamphlets with a partner. Make a list of good points that your partner has made and also anything they may have missed out. What changes could you make to your pamphlet to improve it?

Plenary

If you could interview Matthew Hopkins today, what three questions would you ask him about his work?

WHY DID THE NUMBER OF WITCHCRAFT TRIALS DECLINE AFTER THE 1640s?

By the end of this section you will understand:
- why the number of witchcraft trials declined in England after the 1640s
- how scientific, political, religious and economic developments changed people's beliefs about witchcraft.

You will be able to:
- extract information from a variety of sources in order to answer a specific question.

Starter

Brainstorm a list of reasons why you don't believe in witchcraft.

Why were people becoming less superstitious?

There were a number of important discoveries, inventions and advances made in science during the seventeenth century.

- William Harvey discovered that blood circulated round the body.
- Printing presses made information more widely available.
- The sun was found to be the centre of the universe – people realised that the earth moved round the sun and not the other way round.

- The Royal Society was set up to encourage scientific investigation.
- The first microscopes were used.
- Telescopes were used to look at the moon.
- The theory of gravity was described by Isaac Newton.

TASKS...

1 Why might each scientific discovery described above, and all of them together, stop people believing in witchcraft?

2 Look back at the list of reasons you created as to why you don't believe in witchcraft.
   a) Compare your reasons for not believing in witchcraft with the list of scientific advances.

What does this tell you about why people stopped believing in witches?

   b) Now think about people living in the seventeenth century. For what reasons might some people have continued to believe in witchcraft despite these discoveries?

TASKS...

3 On page 151 you identified reasons why people were superstitious about witches in the 1640s. Now match up the following problems of the 1640s with the changes which might have solved them by 1700. **WS**

Problems in the 1640s

The upheaval of the Civil War had made people scared and uncertain.

Puritans believed that people had to be constantly alert against evil and the works of the devil.

It was difficult to get news and information in country areas.

People were poorer – villages had lost crops and workers in the Civil War.

England had become Protestant. Catholicism had seemed to offer protection against the Devil and sorcery.

Changes by 1700

Protestantism was no longer a new religion. Now Catholicism seemed old-fashioned and superstitious.

Villages had long recovered from the Civil War. People were more settled and were better off.

There had been a secure, stable government for a long time by 1700.

Transport and communications had improved. Country areas were not so cut off from the big towns.

Puritans had little influence in the country any more.

Why were there fewer witchcraft trials in the eighteenth century?

After the 1640s there were fewer and fewer trials for witchcraft. Although some people still did healing and cast spells, this was not regarded with the same fear and suspicion as in the 1640s.

- People understood much more about science – even ordinary people.
- Many machines were invented during this period. People could see that there was no magic in using steam power to make a pump work.
- There were few plagues and no famines.
- Religion was more moderate and reasonable.
- Political events were also settling down – there were no civil wars.

In the eighteenth century the witchcraft laws changed so that it was no longer a hanging offence. Some people still 'dabbled' in magic, however. The last trial for witchcraft in Britain actually took place as recently as 1944, when a woman was convicted of witchcraft under the Witchcraft Act of 1735.

TASKS...

1 Now you are ready to answer the big question about witchcraft:
'Why was there a witch-craze in the seventeenth century?' **WS**

You will need to discuss the following issues and find evidence to support your comments:

- Why were people suspected of being witches? Think of physical appearance and unexplained events.
- What was different about life in the 1640s which encouraged fear and superstition? Think of the political situation and how people were affected by religious attitudes.
- How did witchfinders affect the situation? Think about the fear they created.

- Why did people confess to being witches? Think of the witchfinders' methods.
- What happened to people convicted of witchcraft? Think about the effect of the trials and punishments on ordinary people in a village.

You will also need an introduction and a conclusion.

- For your introduction you might set the scene by explaining about attitudes in the past towards witchcraft and also the views of monarchs.
- For your conclusion you will need to sum up your ideas and reach a judgement about the big question. You might also explain why the number of trials for witchcraft fell during the eighteenth century.

Plenary

Discuss with a partner the plan you made for answering the big question.

- How did you decide what information to put into each paragraph you wrote?
- Do you agree with everything your partner has decided to put into each paragraph? If not, why not?

THEME: SOCIAL LIFE

CONCLUSION

At the start of this theme you probably thought that living Tudor and Stuart times was very dull and boring. You will know now that although their lives were very hard work, often dangerous and sometimes quite frightening, people still had time to go out and enjoy themselves.

People's lives changed dramatically during the period 1500-1750. There were advances in science and the arts, changes in employment, leisure activities and even in the food people ate.

To build up a fuller picture of the times, plot on your timeline important changes in the lives of ordinary people, for example the witch craze of the 1640s. Also, along the bottom of the timeline, make a list of threats and opportunities which faced people in their everyday struggle to survive.

An example has been done for you below.

Ruler	Charles I/Parliament
Main Religion	Protestant
Political Events	Civil War
Changes in people's lives	Witch trials, 1640s
Threats and Opportunities	Threats: Puritan rule

THEME: EXTERNAL RELATIONS

INTRODUCTION

In this chapter we will be looking at the relationship between England and other countries over the period 1500 to 1750. In particular, we will be investigating these key questions:

- Why did England have enemies abroad in the sixteenth century?
- Why were the people of Scotland and Ireland discontented?
- Why did British people explore and settle in different countries in the sixteenth and seventeenth centuries?

Enemies abroad

💡 *What can you remember about the relationship between England and France during the Middle Ages?*

The rivalry between England and France continued throughout the first half of the sixteenth century. During the reign of Elizabeth I, Spain became the major threat. In 1588 the Spanish Armada invaded England and was defeated.

Scotland and Ireland

Religious divisions in Ireland proved to be a major problem for England throughout this period. Various attempts to achieve a peace settlement met with failure and, if anything, made relations between Catholics and Protestants even worse.

The relationship between England and Scotland was also turbulent. In 1603 James VI of Scotland became James I of England but this did little to unite the two countries. A century later the Act of Union brought Scotland under the control of the English monarchy. Would this improve relations?

Explorers and settlers

💡 *Which foreign countries have you visited?*

Nowadays, most people have been on holiday abroad. However, in the sixteenth and seventeenth centuries few people had the opportunity for foreign travel. Two groups of people who did voyage into the unknown were explorers and settlers.

Explorers like Sir Francis Drake were after fame, new lands for England and, most exciting of all, treasure. At the same time, some English people made the difficult decision to emigrate to the New World, settling in what we now call the USA and Canada. They sought a better lifestyle and new opportunities, but often faced a bitter struggle to survive.

TIMELINE
1500–1750

1511–14, 1522–5, 1544–6 King Henry VIII fights wars against France in alliance with Spain and the Holy Roman Emperor.

1557–9 War against France in alliance with Spain and the Emperor during the reigns of Mary I and Elizabeth I.

1577–80 Sir Francis Drake sails round the world.

1585 Sir Walter Raleigh pays for settlers to go to part of North America, which he names Virginia. None of them survives.

1587 Elizabeth I executes Mary, Queen of Scots.

1588 Philip II of Spain sends 130 ships to invade England, but the Armada fails.

1595 Sir Walter Raleigh sails to Guiana in South America.

1600 The East India Trading Company is formed.

1607 The first Europeans settle successfully in Virginia.

1610–11 Henry Hudson searches for the North-west Passage.

1620 The Pilgrim Fathers land at New Plymouth in America.

1642–9 During the English Civil War Irish Catholics rebel and support Charles I.

1649 Oliver Cromwell attacks the Irish town of Drogheda.

1655 Jamaica in the West Indies is captured from Spain by the English.

1664 The English take New Amsterdam in North America from the Dutch and rename it New York.

1670 The Hudson's Bay Company is set up to organise and control trade with the American colonists.

1689 James II lands in Ireland and raises an army of Irish Catholics.

1690 William III lands in Ireland and defeats James II at the Battle of the Boyne.

1692 The massacre of the Campbell clan at Glencoe in Scotland.

1707 The Act of Union formally unites England and Scotland.

1750 Britain gains control of most of North America's east coast.

10

WHY DID ENGLAND HAVE ENEMIES ABROAD IN THE SIXTEENTH CENTURY?

WHY WERE THE ENGLISH SO OFTEN AT WAR IN THE SIXTEENTH CENTURY?

Objectives

In this section you will investigate:

- the reasons for the frequent wars between England and France
- how relations changed between the two countries.

Starter

💡 *What differences do you notice between the map showing Europe in the early sixteenth century and the map of Europe today? Are there any similarities?*

Key

■ Lands of the Holy Roman Emperor Charles V

-- Boundary of the Holy Roman Empire. This was made up of about 300 small states; their rulers were under the influence of Emperor Charles V.

Europe in the early sixteenth century.

A map of Europe today.

Relations between England and France in the sixteenth century

TASKS...

1 As you read the information and sources, decide whether the theme for each of them is:
- land
- religion
- power
- glory
- trade
- other countries.

You may decide there is more than one theme for each source.

You will remember from your earlier studies that England and France often went to war in medieval times. For hundreds of years England and France were bitter rivals and there were many wars between the two countries. The longest war was the so-called Hundred Years' War which actually lasted from 1337 to 1453. Conflict between the two countries continued into the sixteenth century.

The Tudor monarchs of England kept up their claim to the French throne. They showed this by including the badge of the French kings, the golden fleur-de-lys on a blue background, on their coat of arms. Henry VIII's claim was based upon the possessions that he still had in France in the area of Calais.

English monarchs were also keen to preserve the balance of power in Europe. They did not want one country, such as France, to become too powerful as it might invade England. England often sided with other countries to overpower the position of France.

The ambitions of Henry VIII

Henry VII had tried to keep the peace with France through clever **diplomacy** and by marrying his daughter, Mary, to King Louis XII of France. Henry VIII, however, was determined to recover English lands in France that were lost during the Hundred Years' War.

💡 What do you think a diplomat is?

The Tudor royal coat of arms showing the badge of the French kings.

Key words

Diplomacy Managing relations with another country.

SOURCE A

Henry VIII was bent on war – his (Spanish) wife and father-in-law were egging him on, the treasury was full, the country willing, the Pope calling. Henry went to war against France in search of personal glory and for no genuine interests of his own or his nation's.

The historian G.R. Elton writing in 1955.

SOURCE B

Henry VIII's self-imposed task was to solve the Scottish problem. He justified the war as one which was necessary to bring Scotland, in 1542, into its rightful obedience to the English throne.

The historian M.D. Palmer writing in 1971.

Key words

Alliance An agreement made between two or more countries to help one another, usually in a war.

After the Reformation under Henry VIII (see Chapter 1), England broke with the Roman Catholic Church. Henry became the Head of the Church of England, and was no longer 'Defender of the Faith', a title given to him by the Pope. The more England moved towards the Protestant religion the greater the rivalry with France, the leading Catholic country.

France and Scotland were also closely linked. The two countries were often closely allied to one another in the sixteenth century and war with one usually meant war with the other. This influenced Henry VIII's decision to go to war against France.

In 1512, Henry VIII joined with the Holy Roman Emperor in a war against France. It was not a success. Henry's troops captured a town and won a battle known as the Battle of the Spurs, but the Emperor let him down by making peace with the French behind his back. The war proved very expensive and soon Henry had spent all the money left by his father.

The Field of Cloth of Gold

Henry was also interested in diplomacy as well as war and in 1520 he went to France to talk to King Francis I, who was Henry's great rival and enemy. The meeting of the two kings near Calais was known as the Field of Cloth of Gold because they met in one of many tents made of gold cloth. The meeting was a great success - the two kings even talked of a possible **alliance** between the two countries. However, the two kings, apparently equally attractive and athletic, were very jealous of each other. It is said that they agreed to a wrestling match and that Francis threw Henry, who was very annoyed! A return match was never arranged.

💡 Can you think of a recent example of an alliance?

The meeting between Henry VIII and Francis I on the 'Field of Cloth of Gold' in 1520. This picture was painted about 20 years later by an English artist and shows several different scenes.

However, in the long run the meeting at the Field of Cloth of Gold did not lead to friendly relations between the two countries. Within two years England was once again at war with France, this time in an alliance with the Holy Roman Emperor, and King of Spain, Charles. However, in 1525 Henry changed sides and fought with France against the Emperor. He changed sides because he was disappointed with the alliance with the Emperor Charles, who was also the nephew of his wife, Catherine of Aragon, from whom he now wanted a divorce.

There were no further wars between England and France for nearly 20 years, although relations remained strained, especially after the Reformation.

In 1544 Henry's army invaded France and captured the town of Boulogne. The next year a large French fleet threatened the south coast of England, but it was forced to withdraw after a sea battle off the Isle of Wight. During this battle Henry saw the pride of his fleet, the *Mary Rose*, sink suddenly off Portsmouth harbour.

ENGLAND'S ENEMIES ABROAD.

TASKS...

1 Why did England go to war with France?

   a) Decide which of the following are reasons for the wars between England and France.

To protect England from attack.	To conquer new territories.
To make sure that other countries did not become too powerful.	To make sure that other countries did not take over English trade or threaten England's trade with other countries.

To claim lands or titles which had been held by English kings in the past.

To solve the problem of Scotland.

Because the king wanted to win fame and glory.

   b) Put the reasons in order of importance with the most important first.

2 Draw a living graph to plot how relations between England and France changed between 1511 and 1550. Label each of the main events along the bottom of the graph. Put crosses on the graph to show the changes in the relationship between England and France – was it good, very good, bad or even very bad?

EXTENSION TASK

3 Using your graph, write an extended answer to the following question:
How and why did relations between England and France change in the period 1511 to 1550?

Plenary

Look at the following statements and decide whether each is true or false.

- England was constantly at war with France during the reign of Henry VIII.
- The meeting between Henry VIII and Francis I was known as the 'Field of Cloth'.
- England went to war with France to take land from France.

- Henry's wars against France were very successful.
- Henry's wars against France were very expensive.
- Diplomacy means an agreement between two countries promising to help each other.

Make up two statements of your own about relations between England and France. Try them out on someone else in the class.

WHAT HAPPENED TO ENGLAND'S RELATIONS WITH SPAIN UNDER ELIZABETH I?

Objectives

In this section you will try to work out:
- why relations between Spain and England worsened during the reign of Elizabeth I
- why Spain tried to invade England in 1588.

SOURCE A

I write to tell you about my sufferings at sea. The movement of the sea upset our stomachs so horribly that we all turned white as ghosts and began to bring up our very souls. We vomited, we gagged, we shot out of our mouths everything which had gone in during the last two days.

Our dwellings are so closed-in, dark and evil-smelling that they seem more like burial holes, or the caves of Hell. For game in the neighbourhood there are fine fights of cockroaches, and very good rat-hunting, rats so fierce that when they are cornered they turn on their hunters like wild boars. There are lice so enormous that sometimes they are seasick and vomit out bits of sailor.

I see the ship's boys emerge from the half-deck with a bundle of cloths. They spread these out and on them put little mounds of broken biscuit. They would then place on this 'table' a few beef bones with bits of sinew clinging to them. When the meal is laid out, one of the boys sings out: 'All hands to dinner! If you don't come, you won't eat!' In a twinkling, out come pouring all the ship's company saying 'Amen' who, without pausing, whip out their daggers and knives and fall upon those poor bones. It is like an ant heap. Men and women, young and old, clean and dirty, are all mixed up together. The people around you will belch and vomit, or break wind or empty their bowels while you are having your breakfast.

If you want to empty your bowels, you have to hang out over the sea like a cat-burglar clinging to a wall. Your only hope is to wait until you are desperate.

The worst longing is for something to drink. You are in the middle of the sea, surrounded by water, but they dole it out in thimbles, and all the time you are dying of thirst from eating dried beef and food pickled in salt.

A letter written by a Spaniard, Eugenio de Salazar, who sailed across the Atlantic in 1573 in a small ship, *Nuestra Senora* (Our Lady).

Starter

 What can you learn from Source A about life at sea at this time? You could make a list or even draw a picture about what the source tells you.

A historical mystery

Fifteen years later, after his journey across the Atlantic, Eugenio de Salazar sailed on one of the ships of the Spanish Armada to invade England.

- Why did Spain and England go to war?
- Who was more to blame for the war, Elizabeth I or Philip II?

TASKS...

1 a) Re-order the following statements to help you understand why Spain and England went to war and who was to blame. **WS**

a English privateers (pirates such as Sir Francis Drake) attacked Spanish treasure ships.

b In 1559 Philip II of Spain proposed marriage to Elizabeth I, but she turned him down.

c Spain under Philip II was a Catholic country and England was Protestant under Elizabeth I. The English were afraid that Philip would try to force them to become Catholics.

d The Spanish encouraged English Catholics to try to murder Elizabeth I and make Mary, Queen of Scots, Queen of England.

e Spain controlled much of Central and South America. It wanted to keep all of the trade with this area for Spanish merchants only. When English merchants tried to trade with the Spanish **colonies** this led to battles such as the Battle of San Juan de Ulua in 1568.

f After the Battle of San Juan de Ulua, English seamen such as John Hawkins and Francis Drake began to attack Spanish shipping and colonies. Queen Elizabeth I received some of the profits from these raids.

g In 1587 Elizabeth I ordered the execution of Mary, Queen of Scots for her part in the Babington Plot. This infuriated Philip II.

h The Netherlands belonged to Philip II of Spain. Protestants in the Netherlands rebelled against their Catholic ruler. Elizabeth I supported these rebels and, in 1585, sent an army to help them fight the Spanish.

i In 1569 Elizabeth I considered marriage to the Duke of Alençon, who was heir to the French throne and Philip II's enemy.

j In 1587 Sir Francis Drake 'singed the beard' of Philip II by raiding the Spanish port of Cadiz and destroying 30 royal warships and ships carrying supplies ready for the invasion of England.

k In 1581 Elizabeth I passed a law banning the Catholic religion in England.

l The rulers of the Ottoman (Turkish) Empire were enemies of Spain. In 1580 England signed a trade treaty with Turkey.

m In Spain there were a few Protestants. Philip II had them burned at the stake.

n In 1568 three Spanish treasure ships sheltered from a storm in Southampton. Elizabeth I confiscated them.

o In 1580 Philip II invaded Portugal. Don Antonio, his Portuguese rival, escaped to England. Elizabeth I promised to help him attack Philip.

p Dutch 'sea beggars' (pirates) attacked Spanish ships. Elizabeth I allowed them to use English ports.

q France was an enemy of Spain. In 1581 the Duke of Anjou led a French army to help the Dutch. He signed a marriage treaty with Elizabeth I.

r English traders took slaves to sell to Spain's colonies in America (the New World). Philip II had ordered that only Spanish ships could trade with the New World.

Key words

Colonies Foreign lands settled and ruled by people for the benefit of their homeland.

TASKS...

1 b) Now write down why Spain and England went to war. You may wish to organise the statements into categories, for example long-term, short-term, religious, economic and political causes.

2 a) Below are two sketches, one of Elizabeth I and the other of Philip II.

Using the sketches of Elizabeth and Philip:
- Put each of the statements next to the rulers to show who was to blame for the war between England and Spain.

- Any statements which you believe show both were responsible, put between the two sketches. **WS**

3 Write an answer to the question: *Who was more to blame for the war between England and Spain, Elizabeth or Philip?*

Divide your answer into four parts:
- *Introduction*: Set the scene for your answer. In other words, what is the question asking?

- *Why was Philip at fault?*
- *Why was Elizabeth at fault?*
- *Conclusion*: Who was more to blame and why?

 Name two countries that used to be British colonies.

Plenary

Produce two sets of newspaper headlines highlighting who was to blame for the outbreak of war in 1588. The headlines are for:

- an English newspaper
- a Spanish newspaper.

SHOULD THE DEFEAT OF THE ARMADA BE REWRITTEN?

Objectives

In this section you will:
- compare the traditional view of the defeat of the Armada with other evidence
- re-write history.

Starter

The Newcastle Gazette　　　　　　　　　　　　　　　　　　**19 November 2002**

Newcastle hammer Saints 2–1!

Newcastle's title hopes looked rosy after destroying Southampton 2–1 yesterday in a performance that had everything. Despite having only forty per cent of the possession and only 3 attempts on goal to the Saints' ten, Newcastle showed their superiority in the 21st minute when Shearer headed into the top corner of the net. Claims that he was offside were dismissed by the referee.

Southampton were unable to convert any of their seven corners and they had four separate appeals for penalties turned down. When Bellamy went past Bridge and nutmegged Jones for Newcastle's second the game was all over. It took a very muddled goal in the 89th minute to restore some pride to the Southampton team. Comments that the referee was biased were clearly unfounded. The Saints weren't robbed – their finishing was simply poor.

An imaginary account of a Premiership football match.

Read the newspaper article.

 Was Newcastle lucky to win? What evidence can you find?

 Why do you think the newspaper gives this interpretation of the match?

 Now re-write this account basing your version only on the facts and evidence shown in the article.

We have similar problems with interpretations of past events. They are often written to favour one side.

The Armada: what actually happened?

Below is a typical, traditional British textbook version of the English defeat of the Spanish Armada.

A traditional view of the defeat of the Armada, by Historian A

Philip II of Spain sent a very powerful fleet of ships known as the Armada. It was to sweep up the English Channel, clear it of Elizabeth I's ships and then transport his army from the Netherlands to England. The Armada was due to sail in 1587 but was delayed for a year, during which time the admiral in command died. Philip then gave the command of the Armada to the Duke of Medina Sidonia, who had no experience of the sea and proved unsuitable.

The Armada headed for England in July 1588. It was a huge fleet of 130 ships, much bigger than that of the English navy, and was drawn up in the shape of a crescent making it difficult to attack. The odds were very much against England. It took over a week for the great navy to sail up the Channel, and all the time there was a running fight with the English fleet under Lord Howard and Francis Drake.

Queen Elizabeth was not frightened by the threat from Spain and rallied her sailors with a speech at Tilbury in Essex.

The English ships seemed no match for the huge Spanish galleons. In addition, there were far more Spanish sailors aboard their ships than aboard the English ships. On 27 July the Armada anchored near Calais. Lord Howard sent eight fireships into the Spanish fleet at night forcing the Spanish ships to cut anchor and sail out to the open sea. As a result, the faster English ships attacked and sank many of the Spanish galleons.

The Duke of Medina Sidonia had no choice but to sail home round the coast of Scotland. Terrible weather, including strong storms, meant the loss of even more ships. Three months after setting out, only 60 ships returned. The most powerful navy in the world had been defeated by the bravery of the English commanders, sailors and Queen. Spain never threatened England again.

💡 Why do you think Historian A's version of the defeat of the Armada has been popular in British textbooks?

💡 How accurate is this version of the Armada's attack?

Now look at the evidence provided by Sources A–F.

SOURCE A

This expedition is so great and its aims are so important that its leader ought to understand navigation and sea fighting. I know nothing of either. Further, I know none of the officers who are to serve under me and I know nothing of the state of England.

A letter from the Duke of Medina Sidonia to Philip II in 1588.

The Armada, sailing north from Lisbon, ran into storms and had to put into Corunna for repairs. Leaving some ships behind, Medina Sidonia put his fleet to sea again on 12 July, nearly two months after he'd first set sail from Lisbon. The Armada was now 124 ships. When the two fleets met, the Spaniards were surprised at the size of the English fleet and its skilled sailing. The English were equally surprised at the skill of the Spanish defensive formation, forming a crescent. The well-armed galleons were on the wings, and the slow-moving, unarmed supply ships in the centre. Years of crossing the Atlantic and sailing the Pacific meant that Spanish sailors and captains were very experienced and skilful.

An extract from a modern school textbook.

A painting of the Armada in crescent-shaped formation as it entered the English Channel in 1588.

Our council of war had provided six old hulks and stuffed them full of things for burning. They were now let loose, each one directed by a man on board. The tide brought them very near to the Spanish fleet. The burning hulks came so directly to the Spanish fleet that they had no way to avoid them and had to cut off their ropes and so escape in great haste. They being in this disorder, we made ready to follow them. There began a cruel fight. They lost a dozen or fourteen of their best ships, some sunk and the rest ran ashore to keep themselves from sinking.

A young courtier, Robert Carey, was on board one of the English ships and wrote this account years later.

An English painting showing the English fireships attacking the Spanish fleet at Calais, 27 July 1588.

SOURCE F

Since 1577, when Queen Elizabeth appointed Hawkins as Treasurer of the Navy Board, his considerable experience and energy had been used to develop the easily manoeuvrable galleon which had become standard in the English navy by this time. Gun decks were built and the idea of hand to hand fighting was considered out of date. By contrast the Spaniards continued to develop ships which could ram close with the enemy and enable soldiers to board a ship and fight it out. For this reason they carried twice as many soldiers as sailors. Not only this but the heavy Spanish guns had a far shorter range than the English. The major advantage of the English fleet was its ability to hit and damage a Spanish galleon before it got close enough to ram the attacker.

A comparison of the Spanish and English fleets from a modern school textbook.

TASKS...

Compare the evidence in Sources A–F with the explanation of Historian A.

1 a) In pairs, work out five questions that you would ask about how and why the author has interpreted an event.

   b) Share your questions with another pair and see if you can come up with ten questions.

   c) Which are the most commonly asked questions in your class?

ENGLAND'S ENEMIES ABROAD.

173

TASKS...

2 Apply your five questions to Historian A's account. Is there anything from the evidence of Historian A that you would question or change? Here are some areas to check:

- the size of the fleets
- the leadership of Medina Sidonia
- the quality of the English and Spanish ships
- the tactics used by the English
- what happened to the Armada when it sailed home
- the role of Elizabeth I.

3 Historians are always re-writing the past. Have you ever fancied re-writing history? Well, here is your chance. You are Historian B. You have been asked to write a revised version of the defeat of the Armada, which could be translated into Spanish and used in Spanish schools. You should include:

- English weaknesses and mistakes
- Spanish strengths
- examples of good luck.

Plenary

Write down five key words that you have learned in this section.
Ask someone else in your class to define the words.

THE CELTIC FRINGE: WHY WERE THE SCOTS AND IRISH DISCONTENTED IN THE SEVENTEENTH AND EIGHTEENTH CENTURIES?

DROGHEDA: WAS CROMWELL A WAR CRIMINAL?

Objectives

In this section you will examine the evidence on the events at Drogheda in 1649 and make your own judgement about:

- whether the **massacre** at Drogheda was a justifiable act of war
- whether Cromwell was a war criminal.

Starter

💡 *What is happening in Source A?*

💡 *Why might this not be a reliable view of the events of 1641?*

Key words

Massacre The slaughter of a group of people.

SOURCE A

*Driuinge Men Women & children by hund:
reds vpon Briges & casting them into Riuers,
who drowned not were killed with poles &
shot with muskets.*

A Protestant drawing showing the killing of Irish Protestants by Catholics in 1641.

Interpretations, such as the one shown in Source A, are often one-sided and can even be used as propaganda. This shows that studying historical events can pose big problems for historians.

In 1641 an Irish Rebellion took place (see page 48). Irish Catholics, fearing that Parliament would pass anti-Catholic laws, attacked Protestant farms and murdered their owners. Although about 3000 Protestants were murdered during the uprising, the massacre had not been planned in advance. Thousands of Protestants went into hiding, and some quickly took revenge for the murders.

Background to Drogheda

- During the English Civil War (1642–9), the Irish Catholics rebelled. They wanted Charles I's son to replace him as King of England.

- In 1649 Charles I was executed and Oliver Cromwell, a Puritan, became leader of the new Republic.

- By 1649 most of Ireland was controlled by Irish Catholic rebels. Cromwell wanted to gain control of Ireland.

- In 1649 the leader of the Irish Catholics, the Marquis of Ormonde, was in France collecting money and arms to support the rebels.

- In 1649 Cromwell landed in Ireland and went to Drogheda, which was being defended by a friend of Ormonde, Sir Arthur Ashton.

Different interpretations

In September 1649 Cromwell's army laid siege to the town of Drogheda, north of Dublin. Cromwell's army surrounded the town but the local people refused to surrender. When Cromwell's troops finally broke through the town walls they killed nearly all the defenders and many priests, women and children. About 3000 people died during the massacre.

Interpretation 1	Interpretation 2
This interpretation condemns what Cromwell did and says it was wrong.	*This interpretation believes that Cromwell was justified in what he did because of the rules of war at the time.*

TASKS...

1   In groups, look at the evidence shown in Sources B–J on pages 177–8. Which evidence supports:
    a) interpretation 1 **b)** interpretation 2 **c)** neither interpretation?

SOURCE B

You, unprovoked, put the English to the most unheard of and most barbarous massacre without respect of sex and age that ever the sun beheld.

Cromwell told Irish priests that Catholics should be punished for the massacre of 3000 Protestants in Ulster in 1641.

SOURCE C

There are two important seventeenth-century rules of warfare you need to know about:

- A successful army could give 'quarter' to the enemy. This meant the enemy would be shown mercy if it surrendered and gave up its weapons.
- If an attacking army broke into a town and the defenders did not surrender, they could all be put to death.

From a modern history textbook.

Key words

Ulster The most northerly of the four original ancient provinces of Ireland, made up of nine counties.

SOURCE D

A cartoon of 1649 showing St George, the patron saint of England. He is dressed as one of Cromwell's soldiers and is trampling on the Irish dragon.

SOURCE E

I do not meddle with any man's conscience, but if by freedom of conscience you mean freedom to carry out Mass (the Roman Catholic service), I judge it best to use plain dealing and to let you know that it will not be allowed.

Cromwell's views on the Catholic religion, 1650.

SOURCE F

Our army came to Drogheda. On Monday the 9th the battering guns began. I sent Sir Arthur Ashton a request to surrender the town. Receiving no satisfactory answer, the guns beat down the corner tower and opened the walls. On Tuesday the 10th, after some hot fighting, we entered. Several of the enemy, including Sir Arthur Ashton, retreated into Mill Mount, a place very difficult to attack. Our men were ordered by me to put all to the sword.

I also ordered them to kill any people in the town who had weapons. In the church almost 1000 of them were put to the sword. I think that we put to the sword in all about 2000 men.

I think this is God's judgement on those barbarians who spilt so much innocent blood. Also, it will save lives in the future. These are good reasons for what was done. Otherwise, there would be cause for sorrow and regret.

A letter from Cromwell to the House of Commons, written after Drogheda.

SOURCE G

Cromwell's soldiers promised to spare the lives of any who laid down their arms. But when they had all in their power, the words 'No quarter' went round.

Extract from a letter written by the Marquis of Ormonde, 29 September 1649.

SOURCE H

The soldiers threw down their arms on an offer of quarter. The enemy entered Mill Mount without resistance. They put every soldier to the sword and all the citizens who were Irish – man, woman and child.

From a letter written by the Duke of Clarendon in 1668. He was in France with the son of Charles I at the time of the Irish rebellion. He was also a friend of the Marquis of Ormonde, who led the Irish Catholics.

SOURCE I

For the Irish, the way the revolt was crushed was the most important thing. Cromwell said that the massacre would save lives in the future. But in the long run it helped to make bitterness. And that caused far more blood to be spilt. Cromwell's name was branded on the memory of the Irish. To this day, it comes first to mind when Irishmen speak of the wrongs done to them.

From a history of Ireland written in 1956.

SOURCE J

A few years later an English writer, Anthony Wood, described the scene at Drogheda that his brother Thomas had witnessed. According to Thomas Wood, when the people took refuge in the churches Cromwell's soldiers pursued them up the towers, holding the children before them as shields. After which, they went down into the vaults to slaughter the women hiding there.

A version of the events at Drogheda written in 1967.

TASKS...

1 It's decision time! Look at Sources B–J.

  a) List any evidence that you feel is not reliable or trustworthy. Explain how you have come to your decision.

  b) What evidence are you left with?

  c) Which interpretation (Interpretation 1 or 2) do you now accept? Why?

2 You are an investigator who has been sent to Drogheda to report on what took place and decide whether Cromwell was justified in what he did or whether he had ignored **human rights** and carried out a massacre. Put together a brief report in which you:

  • present the evidence for both sides

  • expain how you have reached your conclusion.

Try to use information from the sources you have studied to support your answer.

Plenary

You have Oliver Cromwell in the 'hot seat' and are trying to find out the truth about Drogheda.

• Think of three key questions that you want to ask him.

• Share these questions with someone else in your class. Together, try to come up with five questions.

• Now try your five questions on someone in your class, who will act as Oliver Cromwell.

WHAT CHANGES TOOK PLACE IN IRELAND IN THE 1680s AND 1690s?

Objectives

In this section you will discover:
- what divisions and differences there were between Catholics and Protestants in the late seventeenth century
- how the fortunes of the Irish Catholics changed in the 1680s and 1690s.

Starter

Protestant marchers commemorating the Battle of the Boyne in Northern Ireland.

 Why do people organise marches?

 What does Source A tell us about attitudes towards religion in Ireland?

James II: a Catholic king

In 1685 King Charles II died. His brother, a Catholic, became King James II (see also pages 82–6). James began to put Catholics into important positions in the army, universities and civil service. Catholics in Ireland were given freedom of worship.

In 1688 James's second wife gave birth to a son. This meant that there was a Catholic heir to the English throne. James was over 50 years old and his wife had had many miscarriages, so many people questioned whether the child was really James's baby.

Think back to Chapter 5. Can you remember what nickname the baby was given? Can you remember why?

The English Parliament did not want a Catholic King of England, so it asked the Protestant Prince William of Orange and his wife, Mary, to replace King James. Mary was the daughter of James II by his first wife, Anne Hyde, and she had been heir to the throne before James's son was born in 1688. William landed in England at Brixham, Devon, in 1688 and James fled to France.

The Siege of Londonderry, 1689

In 1689 James went to Ireland and began to raise an army to fight William of Orange. James and his army then marched on Londonderry, which was being held by Protestant supporters of William. The Catholic army surrounded the city. Nobody could leave the town and no food or supplies were allowed in. The siege of Londonderry lasted 105 days during which time the townspeople became so short of food that they ate dogs and rats and drank horses' blood to survive. About 15,000 Protestants died from starvation including nearly all the town's children. Finally, an English warship managed to get into the harbour with supplies and the Catholic army gave up and marched away.

The Battle of the Boyne, 1690

In June 1690 William of Orange landed in the north of Ireland with a Protestant army of 15,000 troops. On 1 July the two armies met at the Battle of the Boyne. William's army was larger and James' army was soon defeated. James fled the battlefield for Dublin, where he told an Irish noblewoman that her countrymen had run away like cowards. 'And you, your Majesty, seem to have won the race,' she replied. James then escaped to France.

THE CELTIC FRINGE.

William of Orange returned to England and left his generals to complete the conquest of Ireland. He then signed a peace treaty with the Irish Catholics in which he promised them freedom of worship and fairer treatment.

However, in the years that followed the Battle of the Boyne, William passed a series of laws against Catholics:

- Catholics were banned from Parliament, universities and the navy.
- They could not vote, run a school or own a horse worth more than £5.
- Catholic bishops were banished and could be hanged, drawn and quartered if they returned.
- Catholics were to lose land in Ireland. In 1688, they owned 22 per cent of the land, but by 1703 they had only 14 per cent.

Plenary

Think of three historical words used in this section, then write down definitions of each word.

Cut out the three words and the three definitions. Ask someone else in your class to match the words to the definitions.

TASKS...

1 Eamonn O'Donnell is an Irish Catholic who experienced the changes in Ireland in the 1680s. How would he react to the above events? **WS**

a) Make a copy of the living graph and plot his reactions with a brief explanation for each.

b) Share your findings with a partner. Do you agree about the positioning of the events?

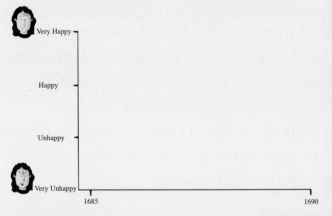

2 Look back at the banner on page 180 showing the Protestant view of the Battle of the Boyne. Produce an alternative view by Eamonn O'Donnell. You could present this as:
- a storyboard
- a mural
- a written interpretation.

WHY DID A MASSACRE TAKE PLACE AT GLENCOE?

Objectives

In this section you will:
- investigate why a massacre took place at Glencoe
- come to a conclusion about the reasons for the massacre.

Starter

Read Source A.

At five o'clock on the morning of 13 February 1692 the signal was given. Two soldiers went into the house of Alexander MacDonald, the leader of the MacDonald **clan**. He rose from his bed to welcome them. Treacherously, they drew their guns and shot him. His wife fled across the room. They shot and wounded her, but she managed to reach the open door. Next day, as she tried to cross the mountains, she died of her injuries.

All along the glen, the silence of the morning was broken by the sound of shots. Clansmen fought with the soldiers to give their wives and children a chance to escape. As the Campbells shot their way from house to house, the MacDonalds fled to the hills. Many of them were led over a little-known track across the mountains. Some of them were to die of the bitter cold. The wounded who were left were shown no mercy. When the soldiers had finished, 38 men, women and children lay dead. The houses in the glen were burned to the ground.

A modern account of the Glencoe massacre.

Key words

Clan A group of people with a common family ancestor, such as the MacDonalds or the Campbells.

Why were clans so important in Scotland?

Have clans existed in other countries? Think about tribes, cults and religious groups. List as many as you can.

What are the modern-day equivalent of clans?

The massacre of Glencoe, as painted by an artist in the nineteenth century.

Solving a mystery

A lot of television detectives solve murder mysteries by looking at clues and piecing together the evidence. You are going to work out the solution to two mystery questions from the evidence which follows.

On 13 February 1692 the leader of the MacDonald clan, Alexander MacDonald, and 37 members of the clan, including four women and a child, were killed.

- Why was Alexander MacDonald killed?
- Who was responsible for his death?

Key words

Highlanders People who lived in the northern and western parts of Scotland. They descended from Celts and Picts who settled in Scotland over 2000 years ago.

Lowlanders People who lived in the southern and eastern parts of Scotland. They descended from Saxons who settled in Scotland around 1600 years ago.

Highlands of Scotland
Lowlands of Scotland

N

Highlanders –
mostly Catholic

Massacre of
Glencoe, 1692

SCOTLAND

Inverlochy
Inveraray

50 km

Edinburgh

Lowlanders –
mostly Protestant

ENGLAND

The division of the Scottish Highlanders and Lowlanders.

The Evidence

a Alexander MacDonald decided to take the oath of loyalty to King William III and travelled to the English fort of Inverlochy to give his oath. He arrived on 29 December 1691, but Colonel Hill said he would have to give the oath to the sheriff at Inverarary, 97 kilometres away.

b One of William III's chief ministers for Scotland was the Master of Stair, Sir John Dalrymple. He believed that the Highland clans ought to be made to fear the law.

c William III signed the order for the massacre. It has been said that the king signed it without reading it.

d The Glencoe massacre was carried out by William III's soldiers.

e The Highland clans were Catholic and had rebelled against William in support of James II in 1689.

f At Glencoe the Campbells broke the Highland custom of hospitality.

g Alexander MacDonald did not arrive at Inverarary until 2 January 1692, but the sheriff was away celebrating Hogmanay (New Year). The sheriff took his oath on 6 January and wrote to Edinburgh explaining why he was late.

h Captain Robert Campbell received the order to kill the MacDonalds while he was their guest.

i The MacDonalds were killed even though they had taken the oath of loyalty to King William III.

j The rebellion of 1689 was crushed by William III at the Battle of Dunkeld.

k Sir John Dalrymple said that MacDonald's oath was a week too late. He destroyed all evidence of the oath and drew up a 'Letter of Fire and Sword' against the MacDonalds. This gave permission for brutal action by the government.

l During the Highland rebellion of 1689, 2000 government soldiers were killed in the pass at Killiecrankie.

m Captain Robert Campbell was sent with 120 soldiers to live in Glencoe with the MacDonald families for over a week. The excuse given was that the fort at Inverlochy was overcrowded.

n An inquiry was held into the massacre but although many of the officials and army officers were found guilty, no one was ever punished.

o William III was merciful to the Highlanders after the rebellion of 1689. He gave £12,000 to the Highlanders. In return, the Highlanders had to swear an oath of loyalty to King William. The oath had to be taken by 1 January 1692.

p Sir John Dalrymple was a member of the Campbell clan

q The Campbells and MacDonalds hated each other and were sworn enemies.

r Highland custom meant that the MacDonalds had to accept the Campbells as their guests. At the same time, Highland custom also said that in such circumstances there must be no fighting.

s William III sent a letter to the Secretary of Scotland on 11 January 1692 ordering him to act against anyone who had not taken the oath. The orders also said that mercy should be shown to those who had not taken the oath, as long as they took the oath now.

t One Campbell was said to have been so sickened by the order to murder a woman and her child in the snow that he killed a wolf instead, then showed his blood-stained sword to his officer to make him think he had obeyed the order to kill.

TASKS...

1 Sort the evidence on page 185 to help you answer the question:
Why was Alexander MacDonald killed?

Present your answer in an interesting format, for example as a storyboard or mind map.

2 Look again at the evidence and produce a written answer to the question:
Who was most responsible for the massacre at Glencoe?
There are several possibilities:
- the MacDonalds
- the Campbells
- William III
- Sir John Dalrymple.

Here is some advice to help you write a good answer.

Introduction
You should write about the argument you are going to make in your answer. Explain the murder of Alexander MacDonald and say why there are several possibilities for who was most responsible.

Four paragraphs
Write a paragraph on each person who might be most responsible. Say why each one might be considered responsible. Use evidence to back up your argument.

Conclusion
Decide who you think was most responsible and explain why.

3 Compare your conclusion with someone else's in the class. Are there any differences? Are there similarities? Why?

Plenary

Have you ever broken someone's trust or good faith? Why? What were the results?

Find two examples of how trust or good faith were broken in the story of the massacre of Glencoe. Share these with someone else in your class. See if you can end up with three examples.

WHY DID THE UNION OF ENGLAND AND SCOTLAND TAKE PLACE?

Objectives

In this section you will:

* investigate the reasons for the Act of Union in 1707
* explore different reactions to the Act of Union.

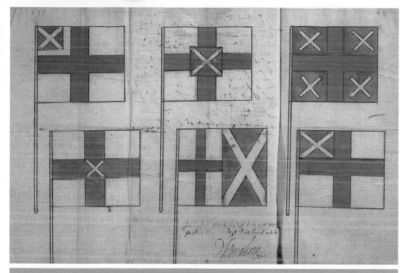

Designs for a 'British' flag in 1707.

💡 *Can you spot the differences between the **Union** flag of 1707 and the one used today?*

💡 *Why do you think that some football teams use the word 'united' in their name?*

Key words

Union Coming together or uniting.

Starter

Look at the designs for a 'British' flag in 1707.

💡 *Which design do you think would have been:*

* *least favoured by the English*
* *most favoured by the English*
* *least favoured by the Scots*
* *most favoured by the Scots?*

💡 *Which design would you have chosen? Give a reason for your answer.*

The 'Union Jack' used today.

Why did England and Scotland unite?

In the eighteenth century the Scots and the English found they needed important things from each other. The only way to get what they both wanted was to negotiate a Treaty, or Act, of Union. Outlined below are some of the reasons for the Act of Union of 1707.

The Protestant succession

In 1701 the English Parliament passed a law called the Act of Settlement. If King William III and Queen Mary, or Mary's younger sister, Anne, died without heirs, then the English throne would pass to the Protestant Sophia of Hanover and her descendants. Sophia of Hanover was the grand-daughter of James I of England (see the family tree below). This line of succession had been agreed in order to prevent there being a Catholic monarch – the throne could have gone to the Stuart line of descent, but the Stuarts were Catholic.

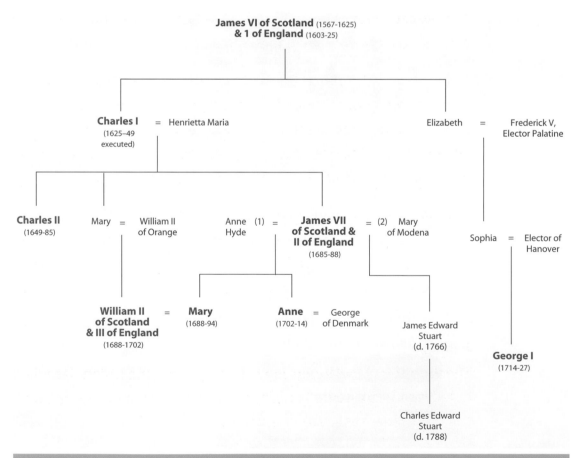

The royal family tree, 1603—1727.

It was vital to the English that the Scots agreed to this settlement. However, in 1704 the Scots passed an Act of Security. This said that the Scottish Parliament would choose the monarch jointly with England, and that the Scots might favour a Catholic successor to Anne.

English wealth

Towards the end of the seventeenth century England appeared to be getting richer. After 1650 English farmers produced more food than was needed and there were no famines. English merchants were making huge profits from trade with English colonies in America.

English laws said that only English merchants (not Scottish) could trade with English colonies. Many English merchants opposed the Union as it meant that they would have to share their trade with Scottish merchants.

Scottish poverty

At this time there were bad harvests in Scotland and people died in famines. The situation was made worse because Scottish merchants were not allowed to trade with the English colonies.

To improve trade abroad the Scots set up their own trading company and a Scottish colony was founded in Panama in 1695. However, English merchants objected to this competition and complained to King William, who used his influence to stop English people putting their money into the new colony. As a result, the Scottish trading company collapsed in 1699.

In 1704 the English Parliament passed the Aliens Act. This said that all Scots would be treated as foreigners and that no Scottish goods could be sold into England until the Scots had recognised the Protestant Hanoverians as heirs to the English and Scottish thrones. This Act meant that some Scottish industries would suffer from competition from more successful English ones.

Religion

The Protestant Lowlanders in Scotland wanted the Union because they hated the Catholic Highlanders more than they hated the English. They saw the Highlanders as savages and thieves.

However, not all Scots wanted the Union. The Catholic Highlanders did not want to be ruled by the Protestant English. A lot of Scots were Presbyterian Protestants and many English people did not support this religion.

Fear of invasion

The English did not want Scotland to help England's main enemy, France. There was a tradition of alliances between France and Scotland and the French could use Scotland as a 'back door' invasion base from which to attack England.

TASKS...

1 Are the following statements true or false? Give an explanation for each answer.
   a) All Scottish people supported the Union.
   b) All English people supported the Union.
   c) The main reason for the Union was the problem of the succession to the English throne.
   d) Scottish merchants wanted the Union so they could share in trade with the English colonies.

2 Write a brief explanation of how you think the following people would have reacted to the Act of Union:
   a) an English merchant
   b) a Scottish merchant wanting to trade with the Americas
   c) a minister of the Scottish Presbyterian Church
   d) a Catholic Highland chief
   e) a member of the Church of England.

3 a) Make a copy of the graph below.
   b) Plot on the graph the reactions of each of the five people.

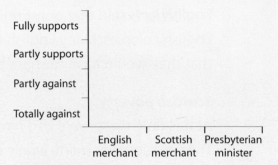

A graph to show reactions to the Act of Union in 1707.

4 Make up two different headlines about the Act of Union for:
   a) an English newspaper
   b) a Scottish newspaper.
   Remember to think of your target audiences.

Plenary

Which of the following words or phrases is the odd one out in each group? Give a reason for each choice.

Group A:	Protestant succession	Act of Settlement	Aliens Act
Group B:	Religion	Highlanders	Presbyterian
Group C:	Union	Coming together	Scottish merchants

Now make up two groups of your own and try them out on someone else in your class.

DOOMED TO FAILURE: COULD CHARLES EDWARD STUART HAVE WON?

In this section you will decide:
- why the Jacobite Rebellion of 1745 failed
- what advice you would have given to Charles Edward Stuart as to how he could have been successful.

Starter

SOURCE A

The Battle of Culloden, painted by an English artist in 1746. The artist is thought to have used Jacobite prisoners to model for him.

SOURCE B

The road to Culloden was full of dead bodies. The Duke of Cumberland (the English commander) stripped the wounded of their clothes and left them with the dead on the battlefield for two days. Then he sent soldiers to kill those still alive. He ordered a barn with Highlanders in it to be set on fire, and his soldiers drove back any who tried to save themselves from the flames.

Chevalier de Johnstone, one of Charles Edward Stuart's soldiers, described what happened after the Battle of Culloden in 1746.

 What can you learn from Sources A and B about the Battle of Culloden?

 Neither source is totally reliable. Why?

THE CELTIC FRINGE.

Why did the Jacobite Rebellion take place in 1745?

There were many reasons for the Jacobite Rebellion of 1745:

- Many Catholics in England and Scotland believed that James Edward Stuart, the son of James II, should be king.

- James Edward Stuarts's son, Charles (see the family tree on page 188), was known as Bonnie Prince Charlie. He wanted to make his father king.

- The Union had not been popular with many Scots. They did not like paying taxes to the government in London.

- In 1744 France planned to invade England, so the King of France, Louis XV, supported Charles Edward Stuart. The French fleet was smashed apart in a violent storm but Charles Edward Stuart decided to go ahead with the rebellion because the French promised to invade later.

(see the family tree on page 188)

Key words

Standard A banner or flag used in battle to indicate loyalty to one army.

Campbells	5000
MacKenzies	2000
Grants	850
Camerons	800
Mackintoshes	800
Frasers	900
Mackays	800
19 other clans	6800
Total	**17,950**

The fighting strength of the largest Highland clans in 1745.

Gathering support

In July 1745, Charles Edward Stuart landed on the small island of Eriskay off the west coast of Scotland. He had just seven men with him but he was convinced that he would win support from both the Lowlanders, who disliked paying English taxes, and the Highlanders, who hated the English. He believed that the clans were just waiting for an excuse to fight the English. In addition, the English had few troops in Scotland so were vulnerable to attack.

In August, Charles raised his **standard** at Glenfinnan on the west coast of Scotland. By this time he had 200 men who were willing to support the Stuart claim to the throne. Charles now set about winning support in the Highlands and was soon joined by some large clans such as the Camerons, the Mackintoshes and the Frasers. The number of his supporters rose to 4000 men.

The Jacobite army exceeded 5500. Of the whole number, not quite 4000 were real Highlanders, who were indeed the strength of the rebel army.

A description of the Jacobite army as it left Edinburgh in 1745.

The Jacobite rebellion of 1745.

The Jacobite army marched to Edinburgh, Scotland's capital city. There were few English troops there and on 16 September the city was easily captured by the Jacobites. With Edinburgh in his power, Charles Edward Stuart expected to double the size of his army.

On 21 September the Jacobites won a great victory against the English army, whom they managed to surprise just outside Edinburgh. Charles Edward Stuart now had two choices:

- stay in Scotland where he was popular and could build up more support
- invade England.

The Jacobite generals advised Charles against invading England, arguing that he would not have much support there. Charles ignored this advice, believing that English Catholics would also rush to support him.

The army when leaving Edinburgh totalled 5500 but at Carlisle totalled only 4500.

Written by Lord Elcho, a Scottish Lord.

Deserters swarm daily from the Highland army.

From the *Evening Courant*, an English newspaper, 8 November 1745.

Every officer, except the Duke of Perth, declared for a retreat. As all the officers agreed in this opinion, His Royal Highness said he would consent to it, though he was much disappointed to be so near to London and yet not in a condition to march forwards.

An account of the meeting of Charles and his generals by Lord George Murray, one of Charles's officers.

The invasion of England

Charles Edward Stuart and his Highland supporters marched south into England. Only about 300 English Catholics joined the Jacobite army and none was important or wealthy. To make matters worse, Charles began to lose Scottish supporters. Some of the Highland chiefs thought that the Jacobite army was too small to fight English troops.

Charles and his army reached Derby, only 200 km from London, on 4 December. Again he was advised by his generals to turn back. Many Highlanders did not want to go any further. They were already a long way from Scotland, they were tired, short of food and freezing. It was rumoured that English armies were closing in, outnumbering them by six to one. Charles had hoped for support from Catholics in Cumbria, Cheshire and Lancashire, but very few English Catholics had in fact joined them.

The Jacobite retreat

Charles and his Highlanders decided to head back to Scotland. What they did not know was that King George II was so worried by the presence of the Jacobite army in Derby that he had packed his bags and was ready to leave London!

The Jacobite army had a terrible march back from Derby and was followed all the way by the Duke of Cumberland and the main English army. On 19 December the Jacobite army reached the Scottish borders. Soon Charles's army grew smaller and weaker. He then made the decision to split up his army to confuse the English soldiers. Even more Highlanders left his army and returned to their homes.

Nevertheless, the main part of the Jacobite army defeated a small English army at Falkirk in January 1746. The Jacobites then reached Stirling but were unable to capture the castle there.

The Battle of Culloden

In April 1746 the Duke of Cumberland and his army caught up with the Jacobites at Culloden Moor, only a few miles from Inverness. At this stage Charles did not get supplies of food and drink to his men so they were half-starved on the day of the battle. The English troops had plenty of food and drink.

Charles again ignored the advice of Lord George Murray, one of his best commanders. Murray told him to fight the English on the mossy, soft ground nearby as this would suit the Highlanders and would be too soft for the heavy English cavalry. However, Charles chose to fight on the flat, springy ground of Culloden Moor.

By the time Charles ordered his tired men to charge at the English troops, the Jacobite army was outnumbered.
The Jacobites were shot down easily by the English –
by the end of the battle, 1200 Jacobites and 76 English soldiers lay dead. After the battle Cumberland's men continued to hunt down Jacobite supporters and kill them. Because of this brutality, Cumberland was given the nickname 'Butcher' by the Jacobites.

What happened after the battle?

The English were determined to find Charles Edward Stuart and crush further resistance from the Highlanders. Many were killed and their homes destroyed. However, Cumberland's men did not capture Charles. For five months after the Battle of Culloden, Charles travelled through the Highlands in disguise. Eventually Flora MacDonald, the daughter of a military commander living on the island of Uist, rowed him across to the island of Skye. From there he was taken to safety in France.

SOURCE G

It was highly wrong to set up the royal standard without knowing that the King of France would assist us. It was a fatal error to allow the enemy such good positions for their cannon and cavalry. The last three days before the battle our army was starved.

Lord George Murray explains why the Highlanders lost the Battle of Culloden in a letter to Charles Edward Stuart dated 19 April 1746.

THE CELTIC FRINGE.

TASKS...

1 What mistakes do you think were made by Charles Edward Stuart at Culloden?

2 Imagine that you are Sir Archie MacPherson, an adviser to Charles Edward Stuart, who has the benefit of hindsight. In other words, you already know what went wrong during the Jacobite rebellion. Write a memo to Charles, just before the rebellion, advising him on how his rebellion can succeed. What mistakes must he avoid? Here is the start:

Memo

To: *Charles Edward Stuart*

From:

Date:

Subject:

I should like to offer you the following advice before you carry out your rebellion ...

Plenary

With a partner, write down what you think are the most important facts about the Jacobite Rebellion. Share these facts with the rest of the class.

WHY DID BRITISH PEOPLE EXPLORE AND SETTLE IN DIFFERENT COUNTRIES IN THE SIXTEENTH AND SEVENTEENTH CENTURIES?

WHAT MOTIVATES EXPLORERS?

Objectives

In this section you will find out:
- why Englishmen became explorers
- what different sources tell us about their reasons for exploration.

Starter

Look at Sources A and B. By comparing the two maps, you will be able to see how accurate Speed's map of 1626 was.

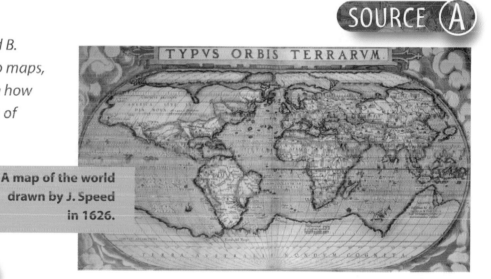

A map of the world drawn by J. Speed in 1626.

A modern map of the world.

💡 Which parts of the world were unknown by Europeans at the time Speed drew his map?

EXPLORATION AND SETTLEMENT.

Why did English people start to explore in the sixteenth century?

The journeys of the great explorers

By 1521 Spanish and Portuguese explorers had found sea routes to what we now call America and the Pacific Ocean. In the 1490s Columbus had sailed to the West Indies and America and, in 1500, he had become the first European to land in South America. In 1498 Vasco da Gama from Portugal became the first European to reach India by sea. Four years later Amerigo Vespucci from Spain explored South America.

By 1550 the Spanish had conquered much of Central and South America. Their fleets returned to Europe carrying a vast wealth in gold and silver. The Portuguese also set up colonies in South America and traded with India and China.

Journeys made by the great explorers, 1486–1580.

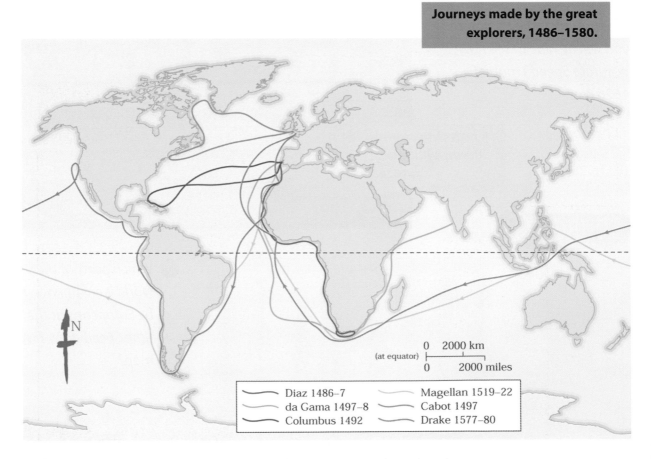

| (at equator) | 0   2000 km |
| | 0   2000 miles |

Diaz 1486–7	Magellan 1519–22
da Gama 1497–8	Cabot 1497
Columbus 1492	Drake 1577–80

TASKS...

Look at Sources C–F.

1 a) Make a list of as many motives for exploration as you can.

b) Compare your list with someone else's. See if you can both add to your original list.

c) Working with your partner, number the motives in order of importance, with the most important being number 1.

d) Write a brief explanation for your choice.

2 Now try to arrange your motives into groups or categories. Give names to your categories.

Our trusty subject, William Penn, who wishes to enlarge the British empire and encourage trade in goods which may be of benefit to us and also wants to make the savage natives more gentle, with just manners and a love of Christian religion, has humbly asked our permission to set up a colony in the parts of America not yet cultivated and planted.

Charles II's Grant of Land to William Penn, 1681.

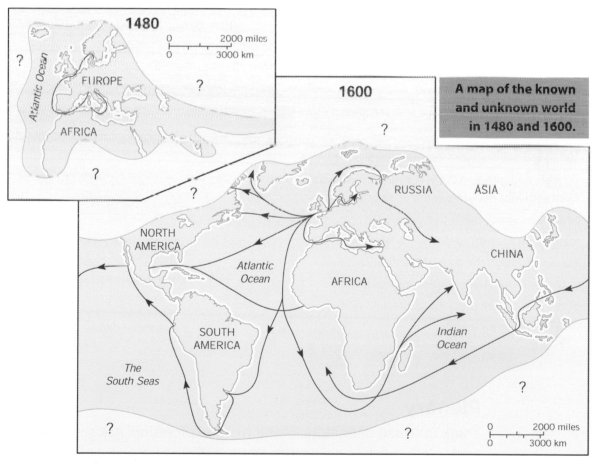

1480

0   2000 miles
0   3000 km

?   Atlantic Ocean   EUROPE   ?   AFRICA   ?

1600

A map of the known and unknown world in 1480 and 1600.

?   RUSSIA   ASIA   NORTH AMERICA   Atlantic Ocean   AFRICA   CHINA   SOUTH AMERICA   Indian Ocean   The South Seas   ?   ?

0   2000 miles
0   3000 km

——— English trade and exploration routes

?   Unknown territory

SOURCE D

The Kings of Spain and Portugal had enlarged their kingdoms. They had greatly enriched themselves and their subjects and had trebled the size of their navies. If we follow, there will be huge demands for English cloth. This will bring great benefit to all those who work in the cloth trade. A great number of men, but also children and women who now have no work, will find employment in making things which can be traded with those who live in the new lands.

Richard Hakluyt, an English writer and clergyman, wrote about voyages during the sixteenth century.

SOURCE E

At first England had been left behind in the competition for newly explored lands in Africa and America. Yet as England grew more peaceful under Tudor rule, men felt willing to explore the world and take the risk of leaving their homes. Merchants were also ready to risk money in fitting out expeditions which might lead to new trade. By the middle of the sixteenth century the English had entered the race to reach and claim lands overseas.

The risk of exploration could bring big rewards. Sir Francis Drake came home in 1580 with loot taken from the Spaniards which was worth half a million pounds. His main aim had been to discover a **North-west Passage** through the seas of North America to the land of Cathay (China) and the islands of the East, where precious spices, silks and jewels were to be found.

From a history textbook, 1967.

SOURCE F

The first and most important task is to spread the happy news of Jesus Christ to those who know nothing of Him. The second is to teach the natives about our knowledge of farming. Finally, the aim is to see what islands and ports you might find by sailing to the north-east, for it would be good that we should have control over our own trade routes to India and China, and so bring ourselves great riches.

Richard Hakluyt writing in the sixteenth century.

Key words

North-west Passage A sea passage along the north coast of North America linking the Atlantic and Pacific Oceans.

Plenary

Think up three definitions of the word 'exploration'. Ask someone else in the class to choose which definition they think is the best .

WHAT MAKES THE PERFECT EXPLORER?

Objectives

In this section you will find out the answers to the following questions:
- What were explorers like?
- What made them want to explore the world?

Starter

- *If you were about to embark upon a journey of exploration, which ten items would you take with you?*
- *Which of these items would not have been available in the sixteenth and seventeenth centuries?*
- *What problems do you think explorers would have faced without these items?*
- *What might they have done to get around these problems?*

The adventures of Sir Francis Drake

Read the following account of the adventures of Sir Francis Drake.

In December 1577 five ships left Plymouth. At the head was the *Pelican*, later renamed the *Golden Hind*. The 164 men who sailed with Drake did not know where they were going. Drake had told them that it was a voyage to Alexandria in the Mediterranean Sea. He knew that many of them would have been afraid to sail had they known the truth.

As they crossed the equator, the weather was unpleasantly hot and the threats of **mutiny** grew. The main plotter was Thomas Doughty, one of the leading officers. Drake ordered the ships to anchor off a deserted coast where Doughty was tried for mutiny, found guilty and executed.

When the ships reached the dreaded Magellan Straits in South America, two of them broke up. The others sailed for 500 kilometres through some of the most dangerous seas in the world. Fortunately, the weather remained fine and, after 16 days, the ships reached the Pacific Ocean.

No sooner had they reached the Pacific than the weather changed. There was a violent storm and another ship sank. A fourth, the *Elizabeth*, lost contact with the *Golden Hind* and sailed back to England. The *Golden Hind* sailed north up the coast of South America and heard that one of the Spanish treasure ships, the *Cacafuego*, had only just left. Drake caught up with it, boarded the ship and seized the treasure chests full of gold, silver, emeralds and pearls.

Key words

Mutiny Refusal to obey orders of an officer.

 What famous mutinies can you think of?

Laden with treasure, the *Golden Hind* set off for home. Drake sailed north to avoid any Spanish warships and eventually landed on the coast of North America, where the town of San Francisco now stands. Here the English sailors met a tribe of friendly Indians who thought Drake was a god and worshipped him. The crew were able to rest and gather fresh food and water.

Drake set sail west, towards the Spice Islands, but the *Golden Hind* ran aground in a narrow channel. Guns and stores were thrown overboard to lighten the ship. Eventually, it slid into deep water. Then Drake set course towards the Indian Ocean and the long voyage back to England. It was September 1580 before they finally reached England. When the *Golden Hind* anchored in the Thames, Queen Elizabeth came aboard and knighted him Sir Francis Drake.

TASKS...

1 Imagine you are a sailor on the *Golden Hind*.

   a) Using the information in the story about Sir Francis Drake, write down the three events that you remember most about the journey.

   b) Share your events with someone else in your class. Have you remembered the same events? Why?

2 Work in groups. You work for an employment agency in England in 1595. Queen Elizabeth has asked you to find an explorer who is willing to search for the North-west Passage.

Read the profiles of the famous explorers on pages 202–5. Make a note of any qualities and characteristics that you think an explorer should have.

Profiles of some famous explorers

John Cabot

Cabot was an Italian merchant who arrived in England in 1494. Like Columbus, he planned to sail west across the Atlantic in search of the Spice Islands of eastern Asia. However, he decided to make the voyage at a more northerly **latitude** because this would make the journey shorter.

> ### Key words
>
> **Latitude** The distance north or south from the equator measured in degrees, for example 45 degrees north.
> **New World** The name for the parts of South and Central America first explored by Spanish and Portuguese sailors.

Cabot needed to find someone to finance the trip. Despite being rejected by the kings of Spain and Portugal, Cabot showed great determination and took his idea to Henry VII of England. Henry had previously refused to sponsor Columbus. This time, however, he was aware of the riches of the **New World** and was eager to support Cabot so that he could profit from the discoveries.

In May 1497 Cabot set sail from Bristol on board the *Matthew*. He showed great bravery in sailing to a part of the world unknown to Europe. A month later he landed in Newfoundland, off the east-coast of Canada, which he claimed for England. He had not found Asia, nor had he found wealth, but he had discovered rich fishing grounds and lands not yet claimed by Spain. Fish was an important part of the European diet and the population of Europe was growing during the sixteenth century, so there was a greater demand for food.

Sir Walter Raleigh in 1585.

Sir Walter Raleigh

Sir Walter Raleigh was one of Queen Elizabeth I's favourite **courtiers**. As well as being a soldier and sailor, he was a clever **orator** and writer. He wrote many poems praising Elizabeth.

Raleigh knew that the Spaniards had found gold and silver in the New World and wanted to do the same. Between 1584 and 1587 Raleigh made four voyages to the North American continent and showed great courage in exploring the coast between present-day Florida and North Carolina. He called this land Virginia, after Queen Elizabeth (the 'Virgin Queen'), and attempted to establish colonies there.

Although Raleigh made two attempts to found permanent settlements in Virginia, neither lasted for long. The settlers lacked the essential food and supplies to survive. They failed to produce enough of their own food or to buy what they needed by selling crops, such as sugar and tobacco. Raleigh was not put off by these failures and brought back to England potatoes and tobacco, which soon became very popular.

Key words

Courtier A person who attends the king or queen in a royal court. Courtiers came from important families and were expected to attend the king or queen at all times.
Orator Someone who gives speeches.

In 1595 Raleigh set out for Guiana, in South America. He was looking for El Dorado, the fabled city of gold, but found nothing. After Queen Elizabeth died, Raleigh's luck changed – James I distrusted him and put him in prison. In 1617 James I gave Raleigh a last chance to find El Dorado, but this expedition also failed and Raleigh was executed.

SOURCE B

Sir Francis Drake painted in c. 1580.

Sir Francis Drake

Drake was the son of a poor farm worker and one of 12 children. He became an apprentice on ships in the English Channel. Once he had served his apprenticeship, Drake began attacking Spanish ships, and gained a reputation as a brilliant and fearless **privateer**. Drake was really more like a pirate, but he attacked Spain, which was England's enemy, so Queen Elizabeth trusted and liked him. He returned to England with lots of gold stolen from the Spanish, which he shared with the queen.

On his return home from his voyage of 1577–80, Drake was welcomed as a hero. A medal was made in his honour and he was knighted. He was only the second person to have travelled around the world. Elizabeth I received £300,000 as her share of Drake's profits from this journey.

Drake bought a big house, Buckland Abbey near Plymouth, with money from his trips. He became Mayor of Plymouth, and then an MP. Drake was very brave: he led attacks on Spanish ships and took great risks to win riches and fame.

In1587 Drake led a daring raid on Cadiz harbour in Spain, where preparations were being made for the Armada. Drake burnt and destroyed valuable supplies and this delayed the launching of the Armada. It was said that he had 'singed the King of Spain's beard'. In the following year, Drake played an important part in the defeat of the Spanish Armada, although victory was probably more due to storms which blew many Spanish ships on to rocks.

Key word

Privateer A commander of a ship who is given rewards by the government for attacking the ships of another country.

In1595 Elizabeth I sent Drake on another mission against the Spanish. He tried to take the island of Gran Canaria, but he was beaten. Drake became ill and died the following year.

Henry Hudson

Hudson was an Englishman and an experienced navigator who wanted to explore North America, especially Canada. He also wanted to find the North-west Passage.

In 1609 Hudson discovered a big river on the east coast of America, which he named the Hudson River. In 1610, showing great bravery, seamanship and determination, he sailed his ship *Discovery* around northern Canada before heading south towards what he hoped would be the Pacific Ocean. In fact, it turned out to be the vast but landlocked bay now called Hudson Bay.

Hudson was not put off by this setback and wanted to sail on, but his crew refused. In June 1611 they mutinied and put Hudson, his son and the loyal members of his crew in an open boat with no oars. They were left to die.

Hudson had explored many areas of Canada which later became English colonies, including Hudson Bay and the Hudson Straits. In later years, the Hudson Bay Company was set up to organise and control trade with the colonies.

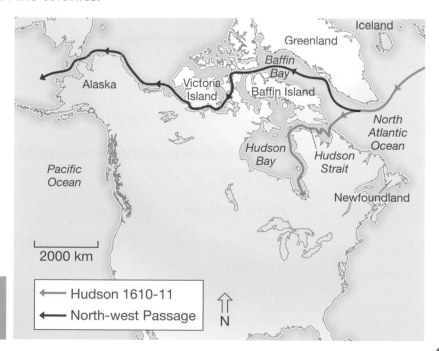

The North-west Passage and Henry Hudson's journey of 1610–11.

TASKS...

1 Use your notes about the qualities and characteristics needed to be an explorer to put together a **CV** that could be used by each of these explorers to apply for the job of North-west Passage explorer. You could do this on a computer. Below is an example of an outline for a CV.

Personal details
Name
Age

Experience

Achievements

Personal qualities

Any other information

2 Each group should now choose one explorer. Put together the information into a CV for this explorer. Remember, you have to convince Elizabeth I that your choice is the best person for the job. Stress qualifications, personal qualities, past experience and achievements. Will you include any failures?

Plenary

Queen Elizabeth I has decided to interview each of the applicants.

- As a class, decide what questions the queen might ask each applicant.

- Agree on three key questions.

- Your group now has 10 minutes to prepare answers to each question.

- Who will the queen choose? Why do you think this person will be her choice?

WHY DID BRITISH PEOPLE EMIGRATE TO THE COLONIES?

Objectives

In this section you will find out:
- what people's motives were for settling in the colonies.

You will also consider:
- whether these motives were positive or negative.

Starter

*Read Source A. William Bradford gives two reasons why people should not **emigrate** to the **colonies**. What are they? Who do you think are the 'wild men' he mentions?*

Key words

Emigrate To leave your own country to go and settle in another.
Colonies Countries ruled by another country.
Civilised A place which is advanced in its way of living.

They had no friends to welcome them, no houses. It was winter, and the winters of that country are sharp and hard. What could they see but a desolate wilderness, full of wild beasts and wild men? If they looked behind them there was the mighty ocean as a gulf to separate them from all the **civilised** parts of the world.

William Bradford, one of the leaders of the Puritan settlers in America, writing in 1645 about what it was like to arrive in the American colonies in 1620.

☀ *What is the opposite of civilised?*

☀ *Would you want to emigrate to somewhere like this? Why?*

Why people emigrated: the evidence

In the seventeenth century many people from Britain went to North America to live permanently on land which seemed to belong to no one. The map on page 208 shows where British people settled in America during the seventeenth century.

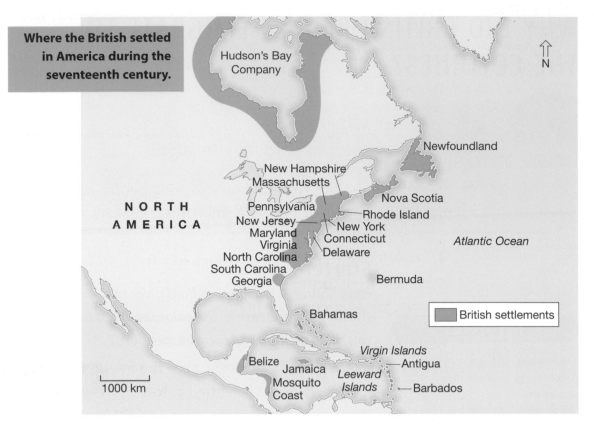

Where the British settled in America during the seventeenth century.

N

Hudson's Bay Company

Newfoundland

New Hampshire
Massachusetts
Pennsylvania
New Jersey
Maryland
Virginia
North Carolina
South Carolina
Georgia

Nova Scotia
Rhode Island
New York
Connecticut
Delaware

NORTH AMERICA

Atlantic Ocean

Bermuda

Bahamas

Belize
Jamaica
Mosquito
Coast

Virgin Islands
Antigua
Leeward
Islands
Barbados

1000 km

British settlements

TASKS...

1 The table below lists some reasons why people emigrated to the colonies. Make a copy of the table. **ws**

2 Use the evidence that follows to make a judgement on the importance of each reason. Give a brief explanation for your judgement.

Reason for emigrating	Strongly agree	Agree	Disagree	Strongly disagree
To find gold and make a fortune				
To make money by selling things to settlers				
To get away from hard work				
To get away from renting farmland				
To find a more healthy place to live				
To find greater political freedom				
Lack of religious tolerance in England				
To do something different and exciting				
To civilise the native people				
To bring Christianity to the native people				
Any other reason				

TASKS...

3 Now separate the reasons into push and pull factors:

- Push factors are negative reasons for leaving England.

- Pull factors are positive reasons for moving to the New World.

Who settled in North America?

Most of the settlers were ordinary working people – farm-hands and other labourers, carpenters, bakers, harness-makers, and so on. They were ready to work very hard and hoped to make a better living in the New World than they had in England. There was a chance, too, that there were fortunes to be made, but many of them had other reasons for giving up their homes.

What were their reasons for emigrating?

Many people emigrated in order to have the freedom to practise their religious beliefs. Puritans settled in New England along the northern coast where there was farming and fishing. The colony of Maryland, on the other hand, was founded by Catholics. The *Mayflower*, the most famous of the emigrant ships, left Plymouth in 1620 with Puritans known as the Pilgrim Fathers on board. However, of the 105 people on the *Mayflower*, only 35 went to America for purely religious reasons.

Others moved to the New World because they wanted to 'civilise' the local population, make them aware of Christianity and even convert them to their religion. They thought that the local people were savages and should be taught European customs and laws.

SOURCE B

It will be to the service of the Church … to carry the Gospel into these parts of the world. What can be better work, and more honourable and worthy of a Christian than to help raise and support a particular Church in a new land.

A Puritan settler writing in 1712.

Many people went to find good, cheap farming land. They could not afford to buy land in England but in America there seemed to be enough land for all. In Virginia, the settlers learned to grow tobacco. Smoking was a new habit in Europe and tobacco was much in demand. Rich 'planters' came over from England and bought up huge areas of land for growing tobacco. Many of them made fortunes.

Some settlers went to the American colonies because they wanted to take part in government instead of having to do as kings and nobles told them. However, many settlers were disappointed as rulers in the New World were sometimes as strict as rulers in Europe, and some officials were even appointed by governments in Europe.

Convicts and vagrants were often transported to the colonies as slaves and servants. After a number of years they were often freed if they would agree to settle in the new country.

TASKS...

1 A group of people has gathered at Plymouth ready to sail to North America. They meet for the first time and explain to each other their reasons for moving to the New World. The group includes:

- a farmer
- a Puritan
- a merchant
- a **republican**
- a clergyman of the Church of England
- an unemployed carpenter.

Put together a conversation between these people and include as many pull or push factors as possible. *Either*

a) write out the conversation

or

b) draw a sketch of each person and use speech bubbles to show what they would say.

Plenary

Write a summary of what you have learned in this section.

You now have a maximum of 30 seconds to tell the class what you have learned.

WHO BENEFITED FROM THE COLONIES AND THE BRITISH EMPIRE?

In this section you will try to find out:

• who, if anyone, benefited from the new colonies

• what the advantages and disadvantages of exploration and settlement were

• how British people gained from colonisation.

Starter

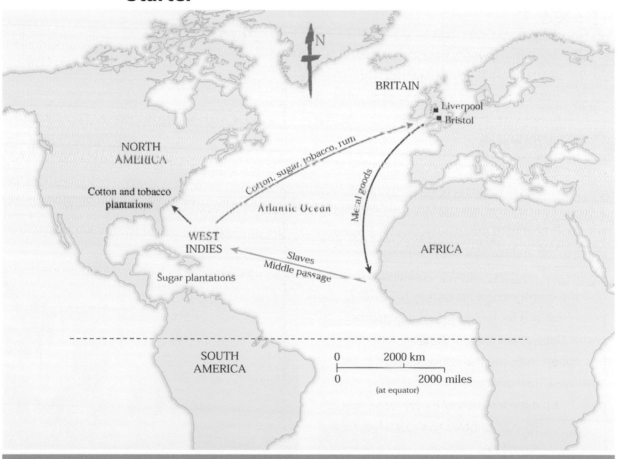

The triangular trade in the eighteenth century.

Draw a triangle to represent the Triangular Trade. On your triangle show the three parts of the trade.

 Why do you think the slave and sugar merchants organised the trade in this way?

What were the benefits and disadvantages of exploration and settlement?

TASKS...

1 As you study the information and Sources A–I, fill in a table like the one below. Show the benefits and disadvantages of exploration and settlement to the British and the native peoples.

Benefits for British people	Disadvantages for British people	Benefits for native people	Disadvantages for native people

A crew of pirates are buffeted by a storm. Soon a boy spots land from the topmast and they go on shore to rob and plunder. They find a harmless people and are entertained with kindness. They give the country a new name, they take possession of it for their king and they murder two or three dozen natives. Ships are sent at the first opportunity and the natives driven out and destroyed. Their princes are tortured to discover gold. This is a modern colony.

An extract from Jonathan Swift's *Gulliver's Travels*, written in 1726.

The dockside at Bristol. In the seventeenth and eighteenth centuries, Bristol grew to become the second largest English city after London. Its prosperity was the result of trade with the American colonies, the West Indies and Africa.

British traders became involved with the slave trade. British ships took Africans as slaves to America. There they worked on large plantations, producing cotton and sugar which were then shipped back to Britain. It was a very profitable business for the British, but at a huge and terrible human cost.

An extract from a modern textbook.

The Africans were so wilful and sad to leave their own country that they often leapt out of the canoes, boats and ships into the sea, and stayed under water until they drowned. We had about 12 Africans who drowned themselves to death, for it is their belief that when they die they return home to their country and friends. Some commanders cut off the arms and legs of the most wilful to terrify the rest, for they believe that if they lose a limb they cannot return home again.

The captain of a British slave-ship, *Hannibal*, describes the behaviour of some Africans about to be shipped to the West Indies in 1693.

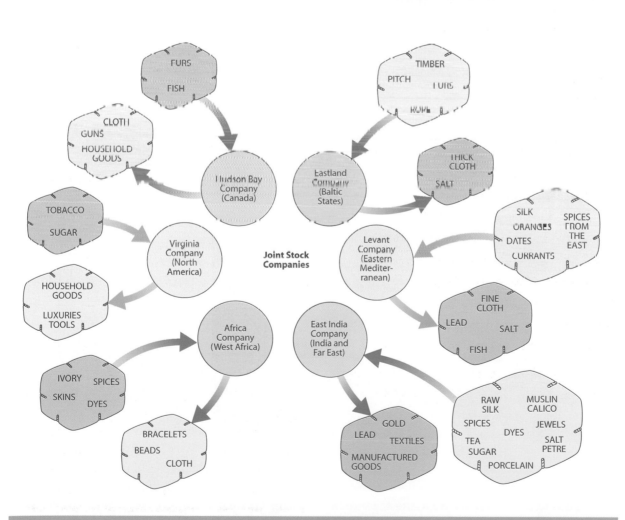

British companies which traded with the Empire.

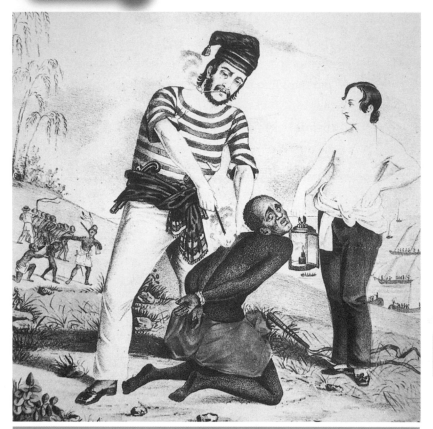

A contemporary drawing of a slave being branded.

The colonies produced new tastes and goods. Sugar from the West Indies, silks and cottons from the East, and spices from all over the world were brought back to Britain. New crops like potatoes and tobacco were introduced to Britain. Tea and coffee had also been unknown to Britain before 1500. The new trade made Britain very powerful and increased its prestige in Europe.

An extract from a modern textbook.

A painting of a coffee house in the seventeenth century. The first coffee houses opened in London in 1652, and in Oxford in 1660.

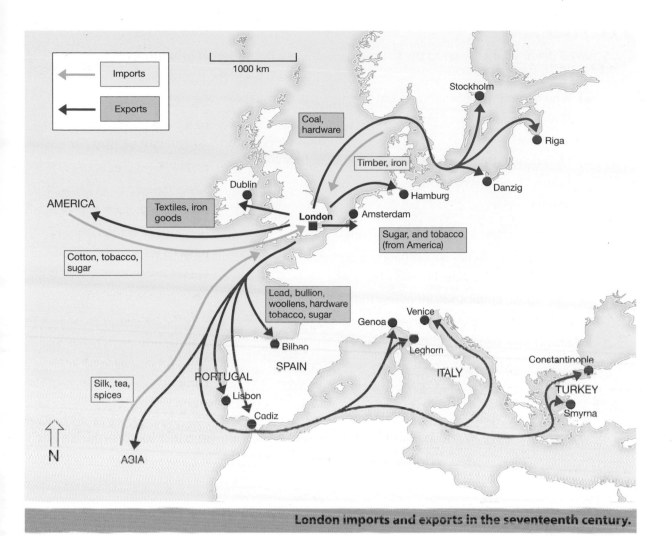

London imports and exports in the seventeenth century.

Owned by James Stone	Value
Thomas Groves, 4 years to serve	1300 lbs of tobacco
Emaniel, a black slave	2000 lbs tobacco
Mingo, a black slave	2000 lbs of tobacco

An extract from a list of the property of the colonist James Stone, 1648.

In Britain, by 1750, you could buy apricots, avocados, bananas, beetroot, kidney beans, melons, peaches, peanuts, pineapples, potatoes, tomatoes, turkeys and gin. The most popular imports were chocolate, coffee, cotton, sugar, tea and tobacco. It became the height of fashion to drink coffee or hot chocolate in one of the new coffee-houses while smoking a pipe and reading one of the new newspapers. Some rich people also had another fashionable 'toy' – a black slave to wait on them.

An extract from a modern textbook.

TASKS...

1 Write down your answers to the following questions:

   a) Who do you think benefited from the British Empire? What evidence do you have?

   b) Who do you think lost out due to the British Empire? What evidence do you have?

2 Imagine that television existed in the early eighteenth century. You are preparing a documentary on the benefits of the colonies and the British Empire. You interview the following people for the documentary:

   • a British merchant
   • a British settler in North America
   • a slave in the West Indies
   • the captain of a slave ship.

   Write out how each might reply to the following question:

   In what ways has the British Empire affected your life?

Plenary

Design a web page that could be used to summarise the key features of today's lesson.

THEME: EXTERNAL RELATIONS

CONCLUSION

Now that you have finished this theme you will have realised that between 1500 and 1750 England's relationship with the rest of the world changed. Relations with Ireland and Scotland went through tense and strained times. Wars were fought with France and Spain. Some of the unknown parts of the world were explored and English people started to colonise the 'New World' of America.

You can now complete your timeline for 1500-1750 by plotting the key developments and changes in England's relations with the rest of the world. You could add them under three headings: 'the Celtic Fringe', 'Europe' and 'Exploration and Colonisation'. When you have finished, use highlighter pens to show whether each of the changes or developments was a success for England, a failure, or neither. Use green for success, red for failure and yellow for neither.

An example has been done for you below.

Date	1620	1630	1640	1650	1660	1670	1680	1690
Ruler				Charles I/Parliament				
Main Religion				Protestant				
Political Events				Civil War				
Changes in people's lives				Witch trials, 1640s				
Threats and Opportunities	**Threats:** Poor diet; childbirth			**Threats:** Puritan rule		**Opportunities:** New industries; growing towns		
Celtic Fringe							Battle of the Boyne	
Europe		War against France						
Exploration and Colonisation	Pilgrim Fathers							

When you have finished your timeline you will be able to see for yourself why these were 'Revolutionary Times'!

Index

V

vagrants 116, 210

W

Walsingham, Sir Francis 40
'warming pan' baby 83
William of Orange, King 82, 86, 181, 182
Wilson, Thomas 27-8
witches and witchcraft
     beliefs in 143-6
     identifying 147-9
     superstition reduction 156-7
     swimming test 153, 154
     witchfinders 150-5
women
     begging 123
     childbirth 106
     place in society 101-9
     rich and poor 104-5
     rights 103-4
     wartime 109